I0470382

Mute Vol 2 #4

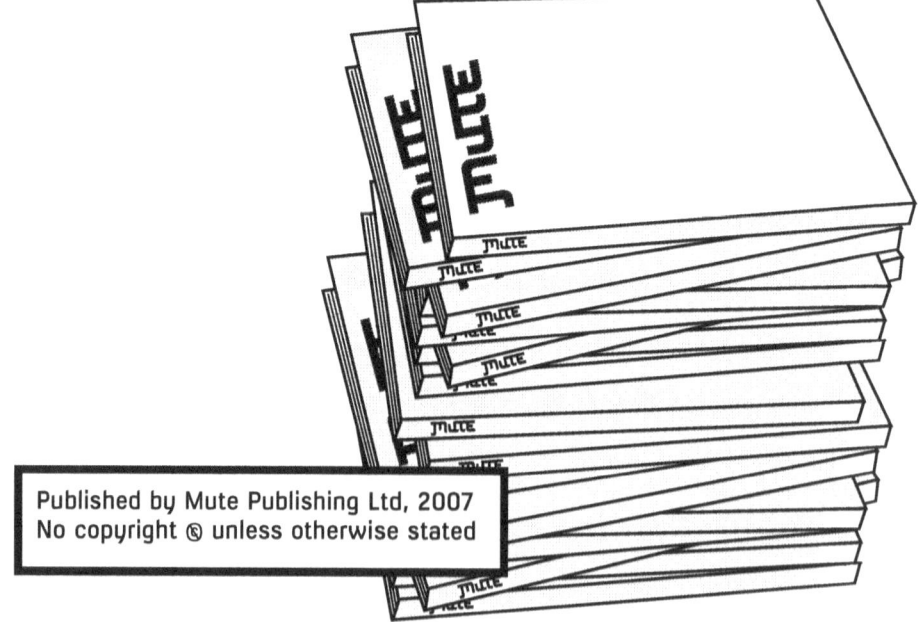

EDITOR
Josephine Berry Slater <josie@metamute.org>

DEPUTY EDITOR
Benedict Seymour <ben@metamute.org>

ASSISTANT EDITOR
Anthony Iles <anthony@metamute.org>

EDITORIAL BOARD
Josephine Berry Slater, Matthew Hyland
<infuriant@autistici.org>, Anthony Iles,
Demetra Kotouza <demetra@inventati.org>,
Hari Kunzru <hari@metamute.org>, Pauline
van Mourik Broekman, Benedict Seymour,
Laura Sullivan <alchemical44@yahoo.co.uk>
and Simon Worthington

PUBLISHERS
Pauline van Mourik Broekman
<pauline@metamute.org>
Simon Worthington <simon@metamute.org>

ISSUE DESIGN
Laura Oldenbourg <laura@metamute.org>
Thanks to Constant VZW for graphics in the
Web 2.0 section

DESIGN DEVELOPMENT
Simon Worthington, Laura Oldenbourg and
Damian Jaques <damian@aant.co.uk>

ADVERTISING
<advertising@metamute.org>

WEBSITE
Metamute.org is powered by Drupal and
CiviCRM FLOSS Software, with additional
software services by our very own OpenMute
http://openmute.org

TECH SUPPORT
Web infrastructure: Darron Broad
<darron@kewl.org>

INTERNS
Special thanks to:
Esiri Erheriene-Essi and Helene Dams

OFFICE
Mute, Unit 9, The Whitechapel Centre,
85 Myrdle Street,
London E1 1HQ, UK
T: +44 (0)20 7377 6949
F: +44 (0)20 7377 9520
e-mail: <mute@metamute.org>

SUBSCRIPTIONS
T: +44 (0)20 7377 6949
F: +44 (0)20 7377 9520
e-mail: <subs@metamute.org>
web: http://www.metamute.org/subs/

DISTRIBUTION UK
Central Books,
99 Wallis Road,
London, E4 5LN.
T: +44 (0)20 8986 4854
F: +44 (0)20 8533 5821

DISTRIBUTION US
Publishers Distribution Group, Inc.
699 Washington Street, Suite 2B
Hackettstown, NJ 07840 USA
T: 001 (908) 813-8511
F: 001 (908) 813-8512

CONTRIBUTING
Mute welcomes contributions of all kinds.
Email <mute@metamute.org> with your ideas.

You can also publish on Mute's website
[http://metamute.org]. Post news, texts,
events and comments, or upload media to the
Mute Public Library: http://pl.metamute.org

The views expressed in Mute and Metamute
are not necessarily those of the publishers or
service providers

Mute is published in the UK by Mute
Publishing Ltd. and printed by OpenMute
http://openmute.org print on demand (POD)
book services in the USA and UK

COVER
Pauline van Mourik Broekman

ISSN 1356-7748
ISBN 0-9554796-1-4

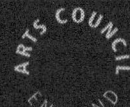

Mute is supported by
The Arts Council of England

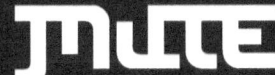

CONTENTS

MUTE VOL2 #4 JANUARY 07

EDITORIAL
by Josephine
Berry Slater

Ever heard of a 'link farm'? This contemporary form of collective farming refers to the bogus population of platforms like MySpace by spammers trying to push their product to the top of Google's search results. Google's page ranking algorithm, Big Daddy, rates the popularity of a page by the number of incoming links it has from unrelated pages on the web. But the loophole is that 'internet neighbourhoods' are categorised into 'good' and 'bad', with sites like MySpace, Wikipedia and YouTube gaining top marks. Spammers fill these favoured sites with fake identities in order to push their wares further up the heights of Mt. Google. According to researcher Sam Vaknin, who has diligently analysed the relation between Google ranking and incoming links, links from MySpace push sites higher up the search results than do any others. Vaknin set out to discover how the invisible hand of Google gives priority to supposedly 'authoritative' sources

such as Wikipedia whose '"editors" are mostly *unqualified* teenagers and young adults'. Like many others, Vaknin is outraged at the implicit shift of legitimacy away from traditional forms of expert knowledge production to social networking platforms. Indeed, the rise of 'Web 2.0' (itself a corporate logo of sorts) has precipitated a new culture war between proponents of 'democratising' mass amateur media and defenders of professionalism and expert research.

Outside of this self-mirroring dichotomy, however, things are more complicated. The cult of the amateur itself is suffused with notions of rights and responsibility. Unlike punk, whose DIY media ethos nihilistically shunned integration, Web 2.0 warriors can be found eulogising 'citizen journalists', 'citizen videographers' and 'participatory citizenship'. Ultimately both pro- and anti- amateurs are defending the same thing – the conditionality of rights. The detractors believe the amateurs haven't earned their right (to create knowledge), whereas the defenders are happy to see

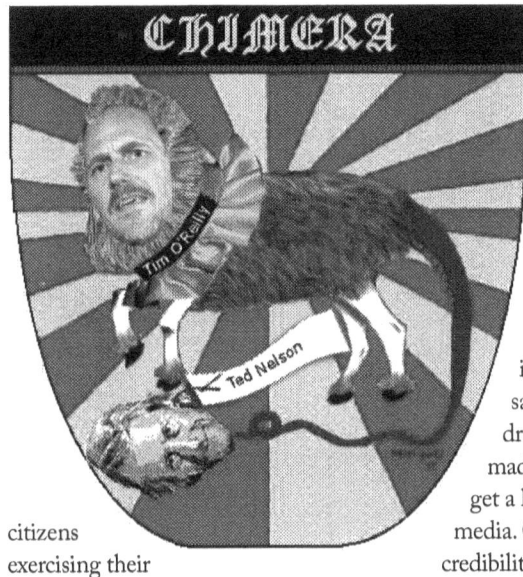

CHIMERA

for commerce as it is for the newly included. Businesses seek to grab the Web 2.0 economy by its 'long tail' (the economic model for sites such as Amazon or Netflix).

Beyond the appropriation of freely produced content by the likes of MySpace, manufacturing the aura of the amateur remains a commercial imperative – like the *lonelygirl15* saga on YouTube where film and drama school graduates created a madly popular mock video diary to get a leg-up in commercial mainstream media. Or spammers who hack the credibility of social networks – a zombie take-over of the 'good' net neighbourhood that is MySpace.

Web 2.0 seems to bring into starker relief the interpenetrating dynamics of chaotic social 'noise', relentlessly systematic search engines, and the centralising drive of commerce. Although criss-crossed with self-defined networks of relation (the trackbacks and permalinks of the blogosphere, etc.), as users we are more likely to navigate with search terms in order to mine the seams of crap and pockets of gold in the datasphere than by other means. Our relation to each other and to the unexpected is largely mediated by Big Daddy and a handful of generic templates. This issue, amongst other things, looks at whether the lashing of Web 2.0's long tail constitutes a real challenge to the old public sphere or its hydra-like reconfiguration. ⟁

citizens exercising their democratic right to free speech. Both imply that with media power comes responsibility – the responsibility to engage in the production of a rational public sphere.

Web 2.0's massification of 'idiot proof' media has undoubtedly produced a plethora of new perspectives and given some of those (socially and/or technologically) excluded from the old public sphere the chance to make their voices heard – or perform karaoke for a global audience. With this entry of the great unwashed onto the media stage comes the possibility of encountering what was formerly screened out of the centrally planned spectacle. Heresies, obscenities, slips, and even repressed truths – the media unconscious is breaking out on our screens. But this, often abject, 'authenticity' is as important

Image: by the Gimp

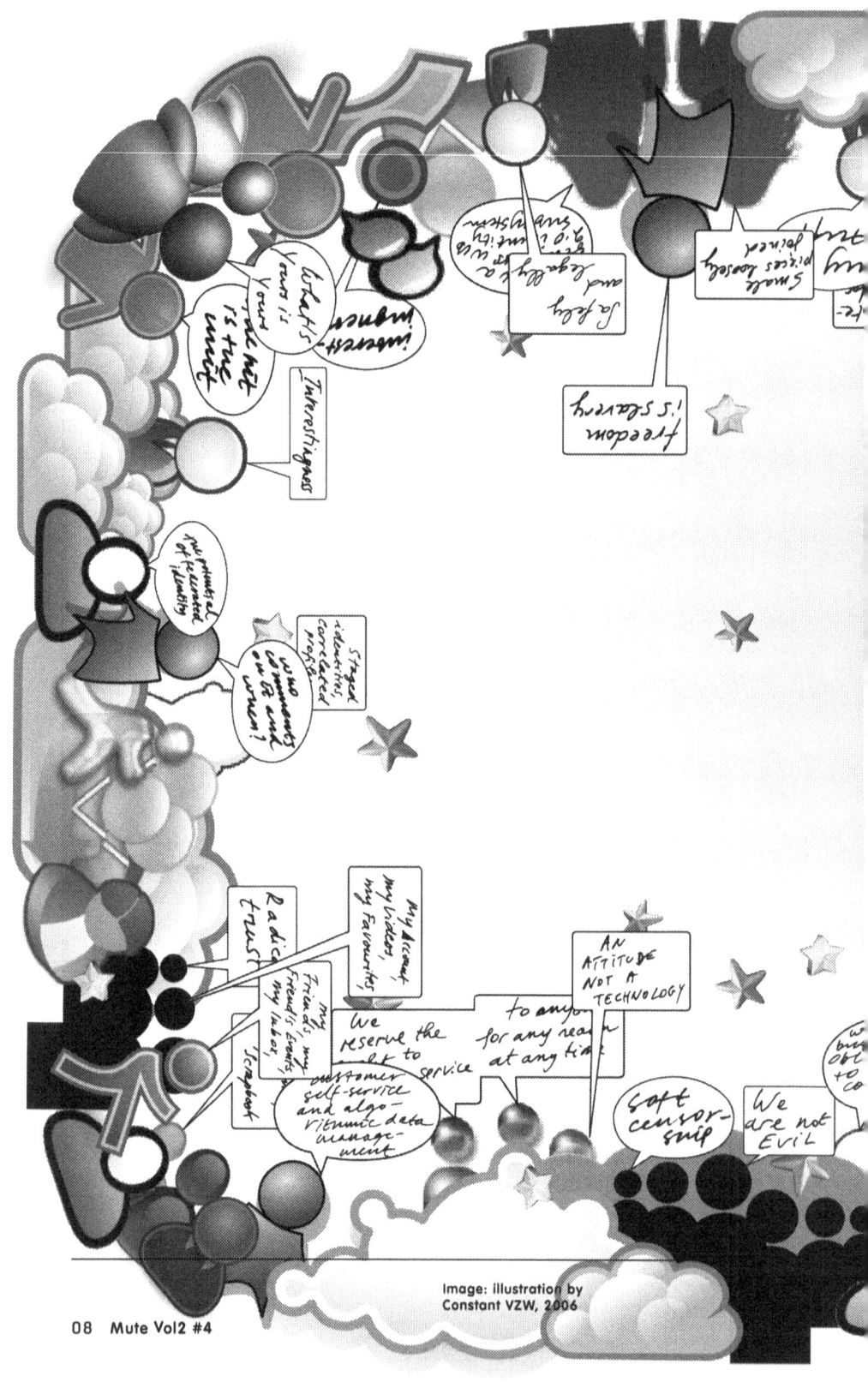

Image: illustration by
Constant VZW, 2006

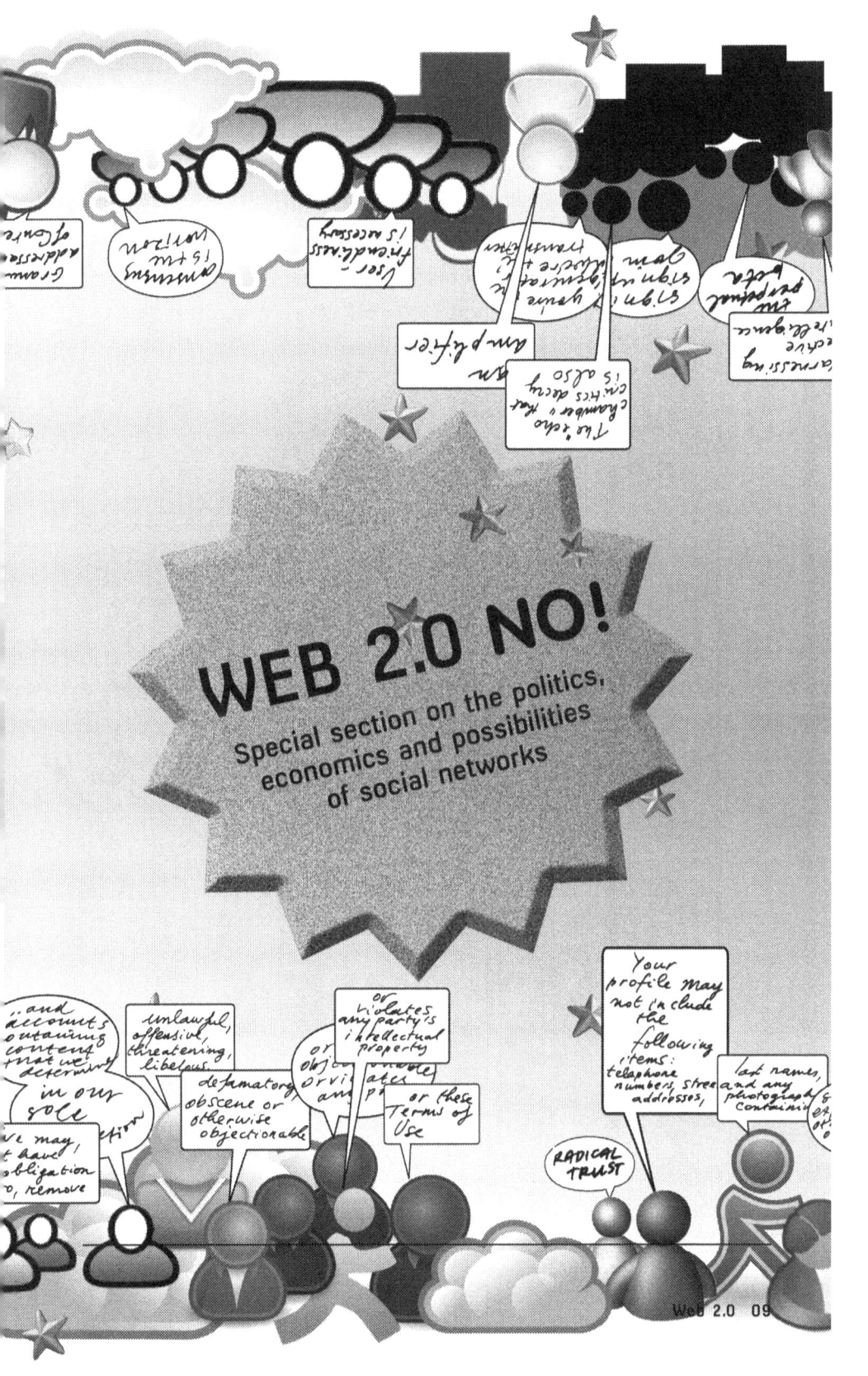

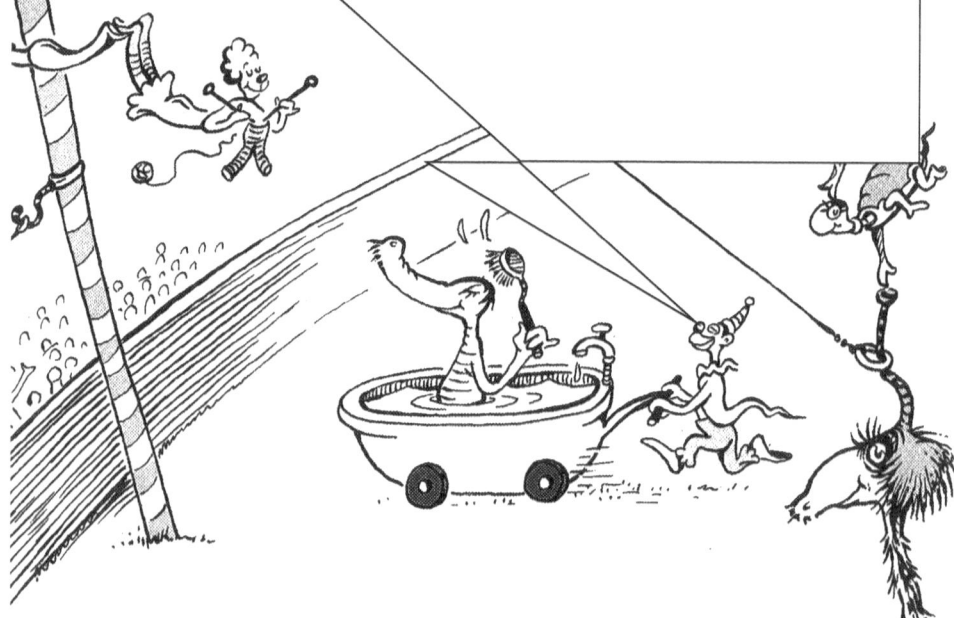

The hype surrounding Web 2.0's ability to democratise content production obscures its centralisation of ownership and the means of sharing. Dmytri Kleiner & Brian Wyrick expose Web 2.0 as a venture capitalist's paradise where investors pocket the value produced by unpaid users, ride on the technical innovations of the free software movement and kill off the decentralising potential of peer-to-peer production

INFO-ENCLOSURE 2.0
by Dmytri Kleiner
& Brian Wyrick

Images: from *If I Ran the Circus* by Dr. Seuss, Random House, 1956

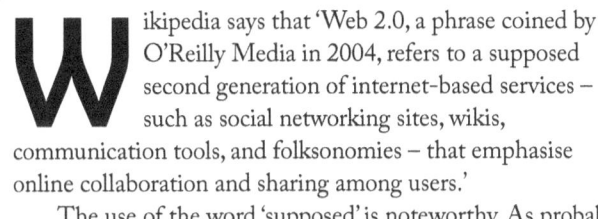

Wikipedia says that 'Web 2.0, a phrase coined by O'Reilly Media in 2004, refers to a supposed second generation of internet-based services – such as social networking sites, wikis, communication tools, and folksonomies – that emphasise online collaboration and sharing among users.'

The use of the word 'supposed' is noteworthy. As probably the largest collaboratively authored work in history, and one of the current darlings of the internet community, Wikipedia ought to know. Unlike most of the members of the Web 2.0 generation, Wikipedia is controlled by a non-profit foundation, earns income only by donation and releases its content under the copyleft GNU Free Documentation License. It is telling that Wikipedia goes on to say '[Web 2.0] has become a popular (though ill-defined and often criticised) buzzword among certain technical and marketing communities.'

The free software community has tended to be suspicious, if not outright dismissive, of the Web 2.0 moniker. Tim Berners-Lee dismissed the term saying 'Web 2.0 is of course a piece of jargon, nobody even knows what it means.' He goes on to note that 'it means using the standards which have been produced by all these people working on Web 1.0.'

In reality there is neither a Web 1.0 nor a Web 2.0, there is an ongoing development of online applications that cannot be cleanly divided.

In trying to define what Web 2.0 is, it is safe to say that most of the important developments have been aimed at enabling the community to create, modify, and share content in a way that was previously only available to centralised organisations which bought expensive software packages, paid staff to handle the technical aspects of the site, and paid staff to create content which generally was published only on that organisation's site.

A Web 2.0 company fundamentally changes the mode of production of internet content. Web applications and services have become cheaper and easier to implement, and by allowing the end users access to these applications, a company can effectively outsource the creation and the organisation of their content to the end users themselves. Instead of the traditional model of a content provider publishing their own content and the end user consuming it, the new model allows the company's site to act as the centralised portal between the users who are both creators and consumers.

For the user, access to these applications empowers them to create and publish content that previously would have required them to purchase desktop software and possess a greater technological skill set. For example, two of the primary means of text-based content production in Web 2.0 are blogs and wikis which allow the user to create and publish content directly from their browser without any real need for knowledge of markup language, file transfer or syndication protocols, and all without the need to purchase any software.

The use of the web application to replace desktop software is even more significant for the user when it comes to content that is not merely textual. Not only can web pages be created and edited in the browser without puchasing html editing software, photographs can be uploaded and manipulated online through the browser without the need for expensive desktop image manipulation applications. A video shot on a consumer camcorder can be submitted to a video hosting site, uploaded, encoded, embedded into an HTML page, published, tagged, and syndicated across the web all through the user's browser.

In Paul Graham's article on Web 2.0 he breaks down the different roles of the community/user into more specific roles, those being the Professional, the Amateur, and the User (more specifically, the end user). The roles of the Professional and the User were, according to Graham, well understood in Web 1.0, but the Amateur didn't have a very well defined place. As Graham describes it in 'What Business Can Learn From Open Source', the Amateur just loves to work, with no concern for compensation or ownership of that work; in development, the Amateur contributes to open source software whereas the Professional gets paid for their proprietary work.

Graham's characterisation of the 'Amateur' reminds one of *If I Ran The Circus* by Dr. Suess, where young Morris McGurk says of the staff of his imaginary Circus McGurkus:

> My workers *love* work. They say,
> 'Work us! Please work us!
> We'll work and we'll work up so
> many surprises
> You'd never see half if you had
> forty eyses!'

And while 'Web 2.0' may mean nothing to Tim Berners-Lee, who sees recent innovations as no more than the continued development of the web, to venture capitalists, who like Morris McGurk daydream of tireless workers producing endless content and not demanding a pay cheque for it, it sounds stupendous. And indeed, from YouTube to Flickr to Wikipedia, you'd truly never see half if you had forty eyses.

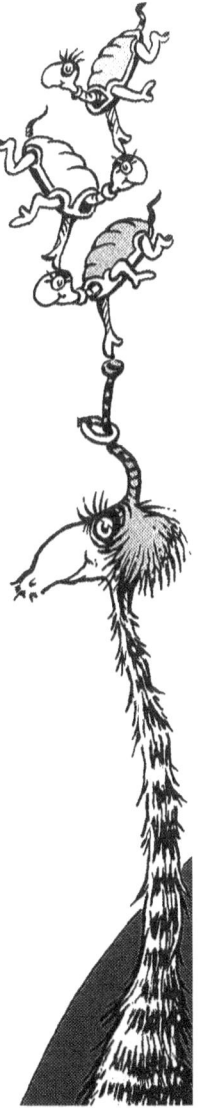

Tim Berners-Lee is correct. There is nothing from a technical or user point of view in Web 2.0 which does not have its roots in, and is not a natural development from, Web 1.0. The technology associated with the Web 2.0 banner was possible and in some cases readily available before, but the hype surrounding this usage has certainly affected the growth of Web 2.0 internet sites.

The internet (which is more than the web, actually) has always been about sharing between users. In fact, Usenet, a distributed messaging system, has been operating since 1979! Since long before even Web 1.0, Usenet has been hosting discussions, 'amateur' journalism, and enabling photo and file sharing. Like the internet, it is a distributed system not owned or controlled by anyone. It is this quality, a lack of central ownership and control, that differentiate services such as Usenet from Web 2.0.

If Web 2.0 means anything at all, its meaning lies in the rationale of venture capital. Web 2.0 represents the return of investment in internet startups. After the dotcom bust (the real end of Web 1.0) those wooing investment dollars needed a new rationale for investing in online ventures. 'Build it and they will come', the dominant attitude of the '90s dotcom boom, along with the delusional 'new economy', was no longer attractive after so many online ventures failed. Building infrastructure and financing real capitalisation was no longer what investors were looking for. Capturing value created by others, however, proved to be a more attractive proposition.

Web 2.0 is Internet Investment Boom 2.0. Web 2.0 is a business model, it means private capture of community-created value. No one denies that the techology of sites like YouTube, for instance, is trivial. This is more than evidenced by the large number of identical services such as DailyMotion. The real value of YouTube is not created by the developers of the site, but rather it is created by the people who upload videos to the site. Yet, when YouTube was bought for over a billion dollars worth of Google stock, how much of this stock was acquired by those that made all these videos? Zero. Zilch. Nada. Great deal if you are an owner of a Web 2.0 company.

unlike Usenet, Web 2.0 is centrally owned and controlled

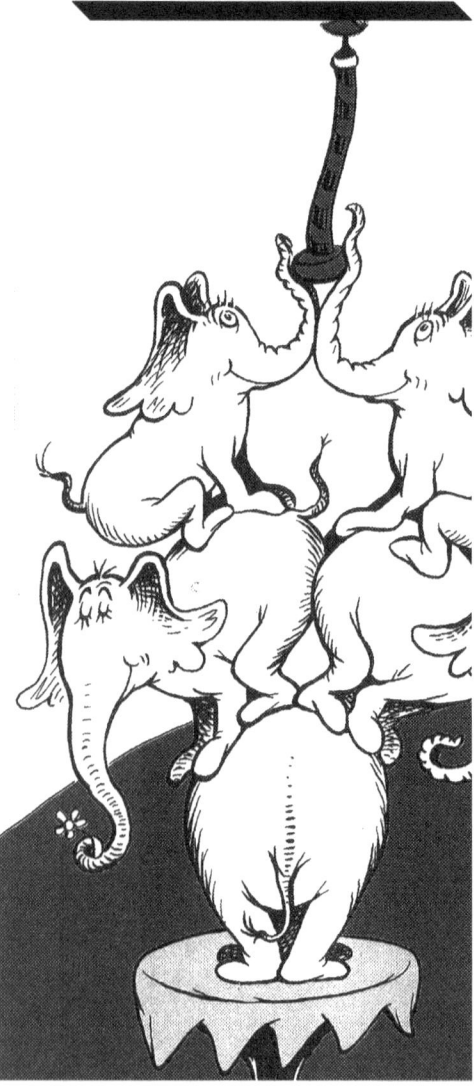

The value produced by users of Web 2.0 services such as YouTube is captured by capitalist investors. In some cases, the actual content they contribute winds up the property of site owners. Private appropriation of community created value is a betrayal of the promise of sharing technology and free cooperation.

Unlike Web 1.0, where investors often financed expensive capital acquisition, software development and content creation, a Web 2.0 investor mainly needs to finance hype-generation, marketing and buzz. The infrastructure is widely available for cheap, the content is free and cost of the software, at least that much of it that is not also free, is negligible. Basically, by providing some bandwidth and disk space, you are able to become a successful internet site if you can market yourself effectively.

The principal success of a Web 2.0 company comes from its relationship to the community, more specifically, the ability of the company to 'harness collective intelligence', as O'Reilly puts it. Web 1.0 companies were too monolithic and unilateral in their approach to content. Success stories of the transition from Web 1.0 to Web 2.0 were based on the ability for a company to remain monolithic in its brand of content, or better yet, its outright ownership of that content, while opening up the method of that content's creation to the community. Yahoo! Created a portal to community content while it remained the centralised location to find that content. EBay allows the community to sell its goods while owning the marketplace for those goods. Amazon, selling the same products as many other sites, succeeded by allowing the community to participate in the 'flow' around their products.

Because the capitalists who invest in Web 2.0 startups do not often fund early capitalisation, their behaviour is markedly more parasitic as well. They often arrive late in the game when value creation already has good momentum, swoop in to take ownership and use their financial power to promote the service, often within the context of a hegemonic network of major, well financed partners. This means that companies that are not acquired by venture capital end up cash starved and squeezed out of the club.

In all these cases, the value of the internet site is created not by the paid staff of the company that runs it, but by the users who use it. With all of the emphasis on community created content and sharing, it's easy to overlook the other side of the Web 2.0 experience: ownership of all this content and ability to monetise its value. To the user, this doesn't come up that often, it's only part of the fine print in their MySpace Terms of Service agreement, or it's the Flickr.com in the url of their photos. It doesn't usually seem like an issue to the community, it's a small price to pay for the use of these wonderful applications and for the impressive effect on search engine results when one queries one's own name. Since most users do not have access to alternative means to produce

and publish their own content, they are attracted to sites like MySpace and Flickr.

Meanwhile, the corporate world was pushing a whole different idea of the Information Superhighway, producing monolithic, centralised 'online services' like CompuServe, Prodigy and AOL. What separated these from the internet is that these were centralised systems that all users connect directly to, while the internet is a peer-to-peer network, every device with a public internet address can communicate directly to any other device. This is what makes peer-to-peer technology possible, this is also what makes independent internet service providers possible.

It should be added that many open source projects can be cited as the key innovations in the development of Web 2.0: free software like Linux, Apache, PHP, MySQL, Python, etc. are the backbone of Web 2.0, and the web itself. But there is a fundamental flaw with all of these projects in terms of what O'Reilly refers to as the Core Competencies of Web 2.0 Companies, namely control over unique, hard-to-recreate data sources that get richer as more people use them – the harnessing of the collective intelligence they attract. Allowing the community to contribute openly and to utilise that contribution within the context of a proprietary system where the proprietor owns the content is a characteristic of a successful Web 2.0 company. Allowing the community to own what it creates, though, is not. Thus, to be successful and

venture capitalists, like Dr. Seuss' Morris McGurk, daydream of tireless workers producing endless content and not demanding a pay cheque for it

create profits for investors, a Web 2.0 company needs to create mechanisms for sharing and collaboration that are centrally controlled. The lack of central control possessed by Usenet and other peer controlled technologies is the fundamental flaw. They only benefit their users, they do not benefit absentee investors, as they are not 'owned'.

Thus, because Web 2.0 is funded by Capitalism 2006, Usenet is mostly forgotten. While everybody uses Digg and Flickr, and YouTube is worth a billion dollars, PeerCast, an innovative peer-to-peer live video streaming network that has been in existence for several years longer than YouTube, is virtually unknown.

From a technological stand point, distributed and peer-to-peer (P2P) technologies are far more efficient than Web 2.0 systems. Making better use of network resources by using the computers and network connections of users, P2P avoids creating bottlenecks created by centralised systems and allows content to be published with less infrastructure, often no more than a computer and a consumer internet connection. P2P systems do not require the massive data centres of sites such as YouTube. The lack of central infrastructure also comes with a lack of central control, meaning that censorship, often a problem with privately-owned 'communities' that frequently bend to private and public pressure groups and enforce limitations on the the kinds of content they allow. Also, the lack of large central cross-referencing databases of user information has a strong advantage in terms of privacy.

From this perspective, it can be said that Web 2.0 is capitalism's preemptive attack against P2P systems. Despite their many disadvantages in comparison to these, Web 2.0 is more attractive to investors, and thus has more money to fund and promote centralised solutions. The end result of this is that capitalist investment flowed into centralised solutions making them easy and cheap or free for non-technical information

Dmytri Kleiner & Brian Wyrick

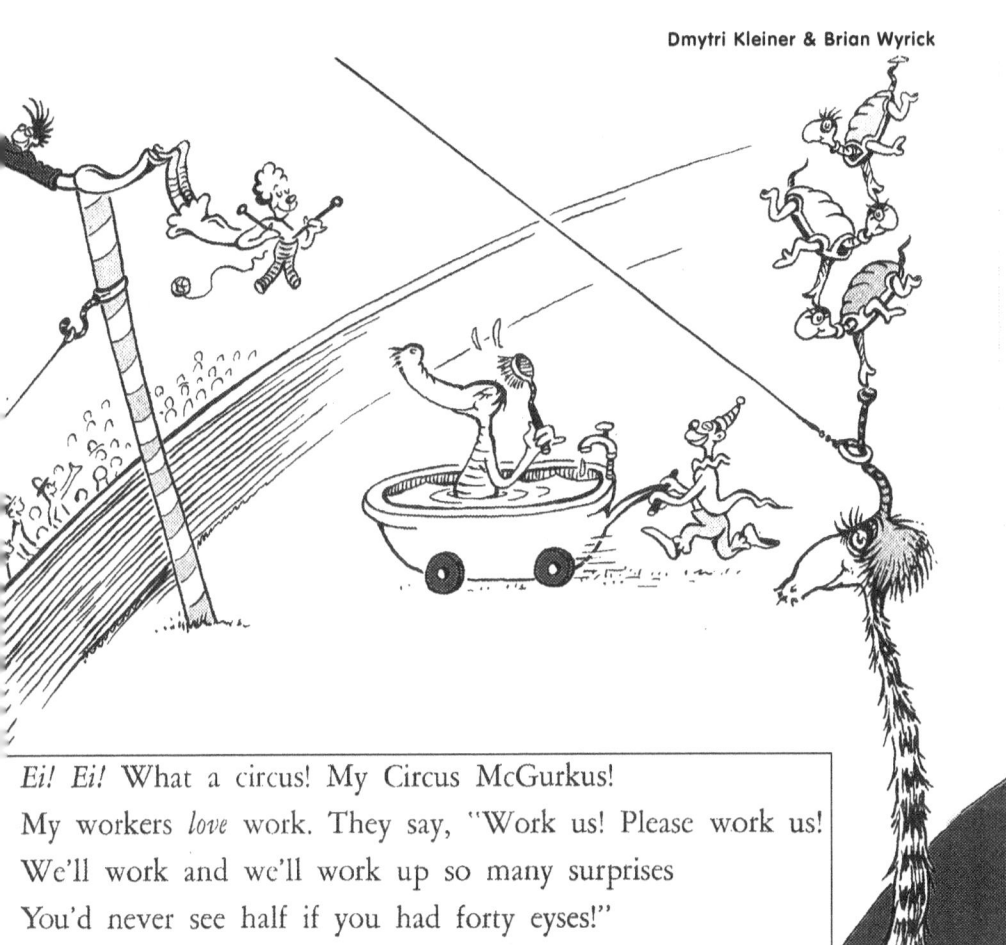

Ei! Ei! What a circus! My Circus McGurkus!
My workers *love* work. They say, "Work us! Please work us!
We'll work and we'll work up so many surprises
You'd never see half if you had forty eyses!"

producers to adopt. Thus, this ease of access compared to the more technically challenging and expensive undertaking of owning your own means of information production created a 'landless' information proletariat ready to provide alienated content-creating labour for the the new info-landlords of Web 2.0.

It is often said that the internet took the corporate world by surprise, coming as it did out of publicly funded university and military research. It was promoted by way of a cottage industry of small independent internet service providers who were able to squeeze a buck out of providing access to the state-built and financed network.

The internet seemed anathema to the capitalist

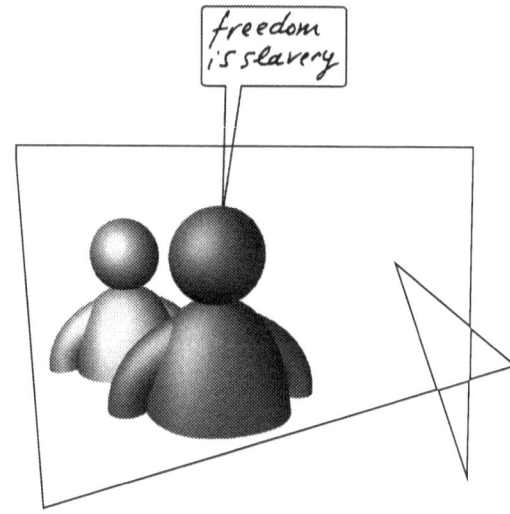

imagination. Web 1.0, the original dotcom boom, was characterised by a rush to own the infrastructure, to consolidate the independent internet service providers. While money was thrown around quite randomly as investors struggled to understand what this medium would actually be used for, the overall mission was largely successful. If you had an internet account in 1996 it was likely provided by some small local company. Ten years later, while some of the smaller companies have survived most people get their internet access from gigantic telecommunications corporations. The mission of Internet Investment Boom 1.0 was to destroy the independent service provider and put large, well financed, corporations back in the driving seat.

The mission of Web 2.0 is to destroy the P2P aspect of the internet. To make you, your computer, and your internet connection dependent on connecting to a centralised service that controls your ability to communicate. Web 2.0 is the ruin of free, peer-to-peer systems and the return of monolithic 'online services'. A telling detail here is that most home or office internet connections in the '90s, modem and ISDN connections, were synchronous – equal in their ability to send and receive data. By design, your connection enabled you to be equally a producer and a consumer of information. On the other hand, modern DSL and cable-modem connections are asynchronous, allowing you to download information quickly, but upload slowly. Not to mention the fact that many user agreements for internet service forbid you to run servers on your consumer circuit, and may cut off your service if you do.

Capitalism, rooted in the idea of earning income by way of idle share ownership, requires centralised control, without which peer producers have no reason to share their income with outside shareholders. Capitalism, therefore, is incompatible with free P2P networks, and thus, so long as the financing of internet development comes from private shareholders looking to capture value by owning internet resources, the network will only become more restricted and centralised.

It should be noted that even in the case of commons-based peer production, so long as the commons and membership in the peer group is limited, and inputs such as food for the producers and the computers that they use are acquired from outside the commons-based peer group, then the peer producers themselves may be complicit in the exploitative capturing of this labour value. Thus in order to really address the unjust capture of alienated labour value, access to the commons and membership in the peer group must be extended as far as possible toward the inclusion of a total system of goods and services. Only when all productive goods are available from commons-based producers can all producers retain the value of the product of their labour.

And while the information commons may have the possibility of playing a role in moving society toward more inclusive modes of production, any real hope for a genuine, community enriching, next generation of internet-based services is not rooted in creating privately owned, centralised resources, but rather in creating cooperative, P2P and commons-based systems, owned by everybody and nobody. Although small and obscure by today's standards, with it's focus on peer-to-peer applications such as Usenet and email, the early internet was very much a common, shared resource. Along with the commercialisation of the internet and the emergence of capitalist financing comes the enclosure of this information commons, translating public wealth into private profit. Thus Web 2.0 is not to be thought of as a second-generation of either the technical or social development of the internet, but rather as the second wave of capitalist enclosure of the Information Commons.

Virtually all of the most used internet resources could be replaced by P2P alternatives. Google could be replaced by a P2P search system, where every browser and every webserver were active nodes in the search process; Flickr and YouTube could also be replaced by PeerCast and eDonkey type applications, which allow users to use their own computers and internet connections to collaboratively share their pictures and videos. However, developing internet resources requires the application of wealth, and so long as the source of this wealth is finance capital, the great peer-to-peer potential of the internet will remain unrealised.

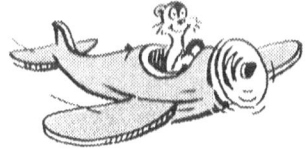

Dmytri Kleiner <dk@haagenti.com> is an anarchist hacker and a co-founder of Telekommunisten, a worker-owned technology company specialising in telephone systems. Dmytri is a USSR-born Canadian, currently living in Berlin with his wife Franziska and his daughter Henriette

Brian Wyrick <brian@pseudoscope.com> is an artist, film maker and web developer working in Berlin and Chicago. He also co-founded Group 312 Films, a Chicago-based film group, and posts updates regarding his projects and adventures at http://www.pseudoscope.com

THE SOCIAL SOFTWAR
by Angela Mitropoulos

Do blogs and social network-based sites offer the prospect of a democratic sociability without borders or wars? Should unpaid producers of content struggle for fair compensation? Or does the very sense of ownership, justice and right founded on labour need to be shaken up?

Angela Mitropoulos takes a critical look at the dissident pragmatism of the startup and the 'alternative' economies of the digital commons

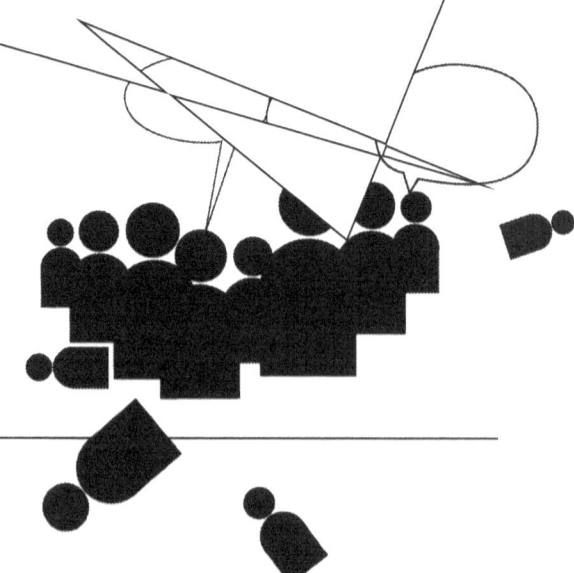

'B eing social' is often understood as the opposite of 'being at war'. 'Social software', even if implicitly, retains this distinction and its premises. Let's begin, then, with the topic of war – and technology. As Clausewitz once famously complained, 'War is regarded as nothing but the continuation of politics by other means.'[1] That is, war is conceived as an instrument – to be defended, opposed, or explained according to ends that are external to it, usually political, but also economic, civilisational, humanitarian, theological and so on. In this sense, war is often reckoned as technology, which is to say, with all the associated connotations according to which technology is considered an instrument. That is, as Aristotle defined technics: a man-made thing, distinguished from man by not having the origin of motion or rest within it.

In another but related sense, the question of war, no less than that of technology, is frequently posed in such a way that the nexus between politics, life and technics is denied – often for the purposes of clinching either a pessimistic or optimistic stance – or credited with an infinite sway. In this way, the question of technology too often becomes, and perhaps parallels, the theologisation of politics (and history) that has repeatedly animated both conservative and radical critiques of capitalism. Whether assigned with almighty powers from which, according to Heideggerian lamentation, 'only a God can save us', or serving as placeholder of eschatological hopes for the reclamation of a divine-like mastery over the world, the question of technology presents itself as the answer to a political question that has – to modify Althusser's remark on the structure of ideology – not been overtly posed. In this respect, Arthur Kroker is right to ask whether 'technology is the name given today to the ancient language of metaphysics.'[2] Foucault's similarly famous reply to Clausewitz – 'that politics is war continued by other means' – suggests the intersection of technics, politics and life as the circumstance of war. Differently put: that war is not outside society, but a condition of it, as an often diffuse and permanent war that, also, marks the perimeter of any given society.[3]

In discussions of the internet, the association between the temporality of this seemingly permanent global war and the entanglements of politics, technics and life has barely begun to be articulated. I want to sketch how this articulation might proceed, emphasising some of the more difficult questions that arise from the intimate networking practices of 'social software', particularly as they relate to copyfights. I am interested in underlining the work dimensions of networking, the implications of always-on net-*working* for conventional distinctions between society and war.

Because work, too, has its theological aspects. From the far-reaching sense of labour as auto-

whether workers achieved the status of human beings was so often a question of whether their labour could be said to be humanising

teleology and auto-production to its specific manifestation in the Lockean doctrine of labour, rights and enclosure, the condition of being at war would be posited as the deficiency of borders and rights. Locke's understanding of society and property rights is of some significance here, being revived in debates over intellectual property, digital content and the like. Locke accorded a privileged status to labour in the definition of the social contract and the determination of rights. For him, the goal of society is the preservation of property rights – and, one can claim rights because labour has been exerted.

Moreover, Lockean arguments are a cliché of anti-piracy campaigns, serving to conflate the work of musicians with the legal ownership of that work by record companies, film-makers with studios, and so on, for obvious effect. But if Locke's liberal contentions have reinforced juridico-commercial property as rightful, they have also been the ethico-political ground of various socialist – from social democratic to national socialist – claims for a properly remunerated labour (or is it life?). Proposals for an 'alternative compensation system' from the 'digital commons' are a version of this; coupling rights and labour together almost as precisely as Locke did. In this way, differences are slid under the equilibriating heading of 'stakeholders' and, as the Berlin Declaration on Collectively Managed Online Rights added, the goal of balancing rights.

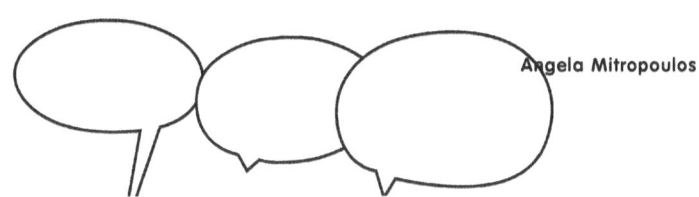

Angela Mitropoulos

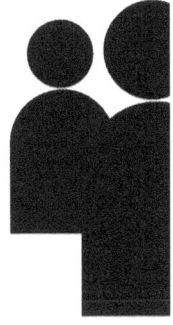

But if one response to this is to insist that there is a crucial asymmetry between wage and profit – without which there would be no profit – the issue becomes complicated if considered through the relation between labour and rights, not least insofar as subcontracting and the 'free labour' of the net serve to diffuse this question beyond that of formal wage contracts. Because it is through the coupling of labour and rights that juridico-commercial precepts radiate as politics and/or morality, which is to say: as the quasi- or openly transcendental determination of merit and its rewards and, not least, justice. For the moment, let's recall Locke's 'labour theory of rights', which is echoed in Marx's writings. Without doubt, entire debates between variant marxisms have turned around the question of this echo. In any case, for Locke, labour, and the property rights that flow from it, are a condition of being human, a secularised version of divine creation. In his *Second Treatise of Government*, he wrote:

> every man has a property in his own person. This no body had any right to but himself. The labour of his body, and the work of his hands, we may say, are properly his.

That is, the human subject consists, above all, in self-possession, in the regard for oneself and one's labour, as property. One can, of course, contract to sell one's labour: 'a freeman makes himself a servant to another, by selling him[self], for a certain time.' A 'freeman', a citizen, is in this sense a proprietor. Locke underscores the sense of the work contract as a non-absolute transference of right and temporal limitation, going on to distinguish servants from slaves. The latter, being captives taken in war, have 'forfeited their lives,' and are therefore 'not capable of property.' The resonances of Lockean justice and right are more than apparent in Marx's writing, not least in the early theme of alienation. They are also, later, much more ambivalently put:

> At first the rights of property seemed to us to be based on a man's own labour. […] Now, however, property turns out to be the right, on the part of the capitalist, to

appropriate the unpaid labour of others or its product, and to be the impossibility, on the part of the labourer, of appropriating his own product. The separation of property from labour has become the necessary consequence of a law that apparently originated in their identity.[4]

Nevertheless, the question of whether Marx, here and elsewhere, adapts a Lockean exposition for the purposes of a subsequent ironic reversal – as in the recurrence of 'at first … seemed' throughout *Capital* – is perhaps less significant than the problem itself. Or, to put it another way: the circumstances and the predicament of the meshing of life, technics and politics that, in later writings and notes, Marx would refer to as 'real subsumption' and, even later still, (translations of) Tronti's writing would emphasise with the concept of the 'social factory.' In this regard, the problem is in no way forestalled by substituting Locke's abstract individual as proprietor with a properly redeemed collectivity of the ergological, productivist society that exhilarated national socialism.

The larger dilemma – aside from the reverence for labour, but bound up with it – is the foreclosure of politics in democratic theology which accompanied the transformation of 'class war' into 'permanent war.' If I put it like this, it is to circumvent the dreaming of a time when war was suspended through the determination of fixed boundaries (not least those

of class understood as an identity) and in the armistice of (social) democracy. While Walter Benjamin's arguments on the author function and technology are important to discussions of net*work*, it is I think his discussion of war that might sharpen the connections between authorial subjectivity, right and war. As he remarked in 'Critique of Violence', war does not annihilate adversaries. On the contrary, war fixes the borders and shape of adversity itself, proceeding to bestow equal rights upon (what is left of) the adversary as contracting party to a treaty. Benjamin adds:

> Here appears, in fearsome originality, the mythic ambiguity to which Anatole France refers satirically when he says, 'Poor and rich are equally forbidden to spend the night under the bridge.'[5]

Borders are not simply geopolitical. They are not only the means by which war is displaced and relocated to beyond socially-contracted space as the division of populations and peoples.

That is, borders are also, in another sense, temporal. From Locke to Marx, the very condition of the ostensible peace of the social contract would be connected up with the temporal limitation of the work contract, in turn constitutive of the difference between the 'freeman' and the slave. But, what happens when such temporal limits are frayed by technics? If I might put it like this, technics 'comes home', as it were.

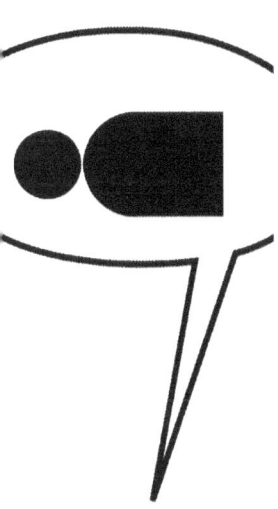

It becomes an intimate *habitus* in the intersection of war and society. Even if this particular war is conducted in more or less soft form, it is as the continuous war of democracy against the outbreak of war within its borders – which is to say, the outbreak of another kind of war, something other than the competitive clash between the formally equal, understood as a prelude to a contract.

And yet, if the proliferation of 'social software' and related copyfights suggests anything, it is that while the concept of work preserves its Lockean associations with right and enclosure, its temporal boundaries give way to an always-on, always available net-working. Some time ago, Tiziana Terranova noted the disaffection of 'netslaves', experiencing '24/7 sweatshops' and 'ninety-hour weeks.' She fruitfully related this to various (post-)*Operaio* concepts such as the social factory, general intellect and, not least, affective labour. For her, the question was:

> How to speak of labour, especially cultural and technical labour, after the demolition job carried out by thirty years of postmodernism?[6]

Mario Tronti explains the problem somewhat differently, less an instance of competing theoretical camps (say, 'postmodernism' versus marxism) than the meshing of politics, technics and life:

> There is a reluctance to confront the bitter theme of the political consequences that the revolution within work has had upon society. The fragmentation of the left social bloc begins with the loss of the centrality of the working subject. This, in turn, was effected technically.[7]

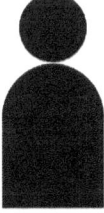

Yet, the 'centrality of the working subject' presupposed certain borders, according to which – to recall Benjamin's remarks – an armistice had been declared and equality bestowed. That is: it is on the ground of the distinctions between paid and unpaid work, the geopolitical divisions of labour, and more besides, that this conjuncture of work and subjectivity occurred and its political centrality was established. Whatever else might be said, the internet is not simply 'animated by cultural and technical labour,'

and not only by a chain of labour stretching around the world that produces, among other things, the chipset and the keyboard. It is animated, should one have occasion to speak of labour and life beyond its anthropological dimensions, by the very impossibility of discerning an originary labour in man. In another sense, and considering the mechanisation of the working body that capitalism puts into motion, Silvia Federici insists that 'the human body and not the steam engine, and not even the clock, was the first machine developed by capitalism.'[8] Further (and Terranova appears to dismiss this question altogether), whether workers achieved the status of human beings, said to possess the very essence of what was said to be human, was so often a question of whether their labour could be said to be humanising.

This is one reason why Lockean understandings of property rights have been revived on the net. As Fred Scharmen notes of MySpace, the 'component parts of the online soul are small pieces of marketing data.'[9] In this shift from habeas corpus to habeas data, which nevertheless maintains the sense of the former as the presentation of the juridical subject (liable to punishment, surveillance, bearing contractual obligation, rights and so on), Locke's abstract individual finds its most cogent expression. Despite all the talk of intangible commodities and immaterial labour as the circumstances that might sunder neo-classical understandings of

property rights, the 'labour theory of rights' has in fact become more, rather than less, explicit. Property in land was never, in fact, conditioned by scarcity (as Johan Söderberg has noted), but by enclosure deemed rightful through the exertion of labour.[10] Locke argued: 'He by his labour does, as it were, inclose it from the common.' Indeed, Locke's argument was, in many ways, an argument for colonisation – alongside Blackstone's *Commentaries*, it became the template for validating colonial property rights. Colonists enclosed the land and made it productive. What counts as labour and production here is, obviously, decided by whether it might be amenable to being counted – calculable, measurable, exchangeable, abstract, parcellised.

And, on the net, the demand that rights flow from labour functions as an insistence that such labour is human labour, after all – that it is not degraded, alienated, etc. Played out along the axes of a labour deemed to have the capacity for self-possession and therefore self-management – especially because of the intersection between language and labour – one can (but not in all cases) dispose of any questions as to what work is by insisting that it means authorship, self-positing, the conscious, reasoned intent that is said to distinguish the work of man from that of bees (or machines). Hence the often intense debates on the net over recognition of authorship and its reward, particularly at the juncture between 'social software' and institutional practice. One can easily recount the instances: anxieties and musings about whether blogs amount to proper (academic) work which may, therefore, be appropriated by oneself or others (either copyrighted, attached to a CV or 'stolen'); whether *Battlestar Galactica* webisodes were promotional material or creditable parts of the series; and, following from this, whether the work of fansites, blogs and wikis are promotional material which rightfully can be (as occurred with fandom.com) managed by studios.

Likewise, remunerated or not by actual money, it would be absurd to suggest that exchange and competition – not least in their democratic register – have not predominated as expectation or model on the net, albeit in a particularly intimate and self-managed form. Even where utopian possibility was pronounced in proto-communist terms, the elaboration of a 'gift economy' as an economy – that is, marked by exchange, reciprocity and contract – suggested that much of the gifting was perhaps the surreptitious anticipation of reward and, so, hardly a gift at all.[11] Therefore, the invention of the term 'Web 2.0' merely provides a handy label for processes that have been occurring for some time. It also makes apparent certain assumptions about net*work* as confined to and having the character of intellectual work. Tim O'Reilly explicitly stated that 'Web 2.0' is the 'harnessing of collective intelligence.' Henry Jenkins asked:

> if these grassroots efforts [of fansites, social software and suchlike] are generating value (and in fact, wealth) and their creative power is being tapped by major corporations, at what point should they start receiving a share of revenue for their work?[12]

Leaving aside the questions this raises about corporate control over such efforts, where does one locate the 'origin' of such creativity, since the proposition of creativity so often assumes an originary (and often individuated) authorship? There is a prelude to this. Laments over the degradation of human labour through technics turns out to be the reassertion of a recent and relative privilege (of so-called 'creative work') deemed lost. And it is in that process of mourning that a more intense recourse to the language of credit, right and authorship has occurred. Flattened into the language of an unperturbed 'immanence', such mourning can segue into an appeal for a properly self-managed labour and the celebration of a coming ergological society – a renewed productivist vitalism that regains the centrality of the concept of labour by conceding that while everything might be becoming laborious, 'work makes free', or it could.

It did not take long, for instance, for the political valorisations of, say, immaterial workers as the new revolutionary subject to shift into an explicitly hipster-entrepreneurial gear, notable in Richard Florida's talk of the 'creative class'. Alongside these revivals of Lockean notions of property, labour and right on the net, there are increasing and predictable suggestions to 'switch off'. Displacing questions about work into fears of technology as an 'inhuman force', the tendency here is toward moral panics and the proliferation of surveillance and control (mostly of children), and often through software (such as i-Kids mobile phones with a parent-prescribed set of numbers that can be received or dialled and which can act as a leash to Government-subsidised distributions of 'net nanny').

Therefore, it may be better to ask what technology's displacement and dispersion of work might mean for reformulating the very sense of work itself, against concepts of work as appropriation of the world, or work of one's self (self-positing and self-possession), or work as the rejection of what is deemed foreign, including what is regarded (as Werner Hamacher argues) as 'foreign to work.'[13] That is, all along the various registers of not-work, not proper work, inappropriate and inappropriable, unemployed, populations deemed superfluous, propertyless, without value – 'what in work does not correspond to an ergological figure … and does not come back to itself.' Undoubtedly, there are aspects of net-work that are significant in this respect: from the 'wasting of time' at work in the form of 'notworking', to the risk that 'exposure' on the net might overflow, depose or even expose its (self-)marketing aspects.

And so, the political question which I alluded to earlier – the question that is not posed by presenting it as a *question of technology* – is not that of reinstating the nobility of politics – or humanity – over technics, along the lines of, say, Andrew Feenberg's arguments for democratic control over technology, or Graham Longford's calls for a 'democratic reinvention of cyberspace.'[14] Nor, along similar lines, is it a matter of suggesting that the invocation of 'the YouTube community' in the announcement of YouTube's sale to Google was the cynical deployment of sociality for commercial appropriation, as John McMurria has argued.[15] Contrary to McMurria and others, neither democracy nor community nor society can exist without recourse to borders and, in each of those cases, the mythologised semblance (and therefore denial) of those borders. Particularly with democracy, juridico-commercial subjectivity is conceived as the very idea of political subjectivity, right down into the confluences between equality and abstract labour and the structural rifts they are constituted through: that is, inequality and concrete indifference.

Indeed, insofar as blogs and other 'user-generated' sites assume the model of democracy or community, the question of exclusion (of what/who is included and

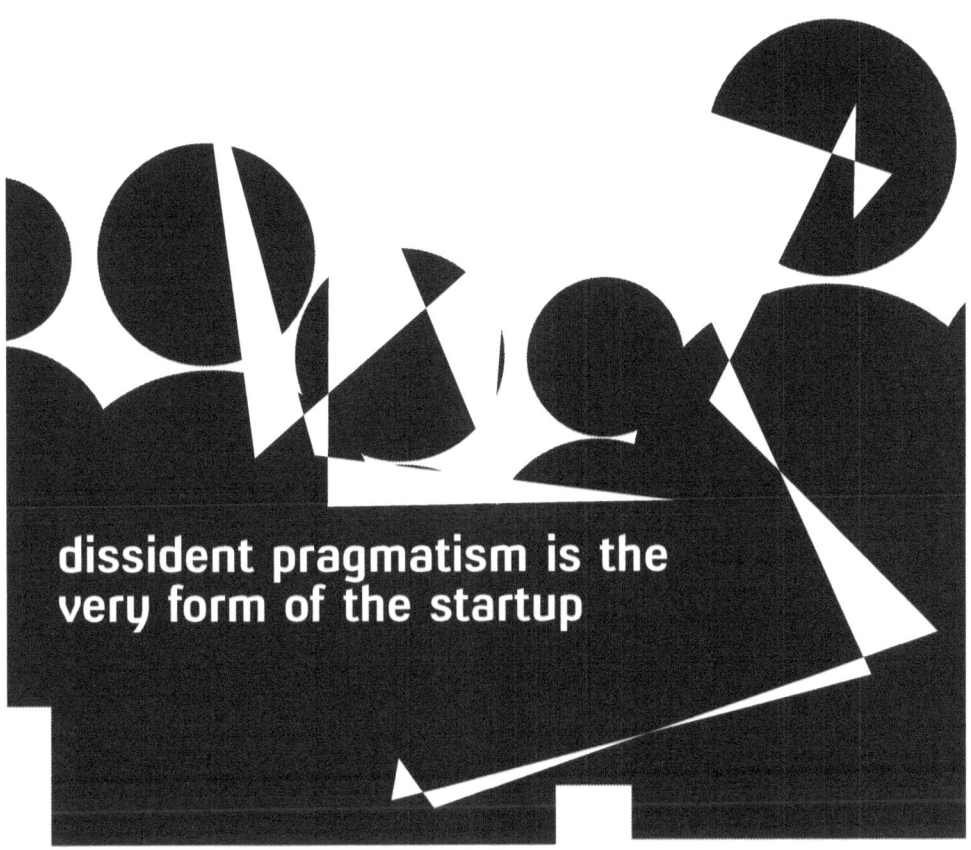

dissident pragmatism is the very form of the startup

what/who is not), becomes depoliticised. That is, less a question of differences than numerical calculations. Thus, the purportedly open character of blogs and social networks takes its cue from money as the universal equivalent, assuming the same structure of concrete indifference (and exclusion). It is no coincidence that one 'how to blog successfully' site recommends regarding blogs as pieces of 'real estate' – the model of landed property is insistent. Even if such property is digital, it is made intimate, as the technics of self – and through the conduit of a 'labour theory of right.' In this way, relation, and non-relation, are no longer questions, an experiment in politics, but a market to be expanded.

The specificity of the political, then, is difference – but it is also the cut of difference that can, perhaps, cut both ways. But it will have to be politics conceived otherwise. Neither the difference of competition which puts difference *to work*. Nor the difference of a dialectics which *works out* differences. Nor, for that matter the difference as the work of self (as in Schmitt's existential theology of friend and enemy, toiling on the vocabularies and borders of identity and self-determination). On the contrary, it will have to be difference and relation posed as a question, each time. To be sure, the argument which follows cannot be that people should not be paid, or have an income. But this is not an ontological predicament. Aestheticisations of poverty are no less theological or odious than is Protestantism's work ethic. Rather, conflicts on the net, as elsewhere, need not continue to have recourse to a labour theory of rights to be political struggles. What is at stake here is by no means confined to the internet. Which is to say: it is no coincidence that migration is increasingly and explicitly controlled through reference to labour. From Bush's insistence that undocumented migrants must 'earn' an amnesty, to the coupling of work contracts and legalisation in the EU, the connection between the emerging criteria of 'netizenship' and citizenship are yet to be detailed in their connections, but those connections are pronounced.

Struggles need not posit labour as a condition of right – or, for that matter, understand labour as a condition of life – even as the meshing of technics, life and politics cannot be denied. Which is to say: there is an impasse here, which needs to be cut through. And no amount of pragmatism, in the demand for, say, just compensation can turn aside from its pragmatic repercussions: not least the validation of a border between ostensibly contractarian, self-managed subjects and those deemed incapable of contracting and therefore lacking subjectivity itself (i.e., treated as things, *pragma*). [For more on these aspects, see Angela Mitropoulos, 'Under the Beach, the Barbed Wire' in *Mute* Vol2#2] This is the condition of post-Fordist policing (or is it a war?).

Moreover, as Adorno and Horkheimer remarked, 'Realistic dissidence is the trademark of anyone who has a new idea in business.'[16] One could add that dissident pragmatism is the very form of the startup. Unquestionably, without work life would grind to a halt, but life does indeed grind to a halt in so many ways that the question of what is life and what is labour (and for whom does the adhesion of labour as life become a condition of life or threat of death) should become *the* questions.

There are various ways such differences can be played out, perhaps as the difference between wage and profit, even as this unravels in some cases through subcontracting and so on. Or, more 'creatively', in the difference between the 'creative commons' (of subjects defined as authors) and the undercommons – of those who no longer, if indeed they ever did, figure politically as workers; deemed not to have the origin of movement within themselves, mere prostheses of 'creative' labour taking place elsewhere.[17] Or, in a more complex way, through the difference between 'here and now' conflicts over digital content and the insistence that technology is the historical repository of 'dead labour' as Marx suggested (and an archive, as Derrida argued[18]) and, therefore, what amounts to the incalculable justification of filesharing, editing and reprisal. Yet whatever the particular lines drawn in this other kind of softwar might be, politics here will be a matter of working through the question of work itself, in its differences.

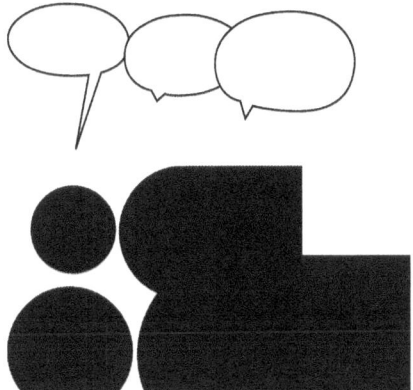

Footnotes

1
Sun Tzu, *On War*, 1873.

2
Arthur Kroker, *Born Again Ideology: Religion, Technology, and Terrorism*, 2006.

3
Michel Foucault, '*Society Must Be Defended': Lectures at the College de France, 1976-76* (Trans) David Macey; (Eds) Mauro Bertani and Alessandro Fontana, Picador, 2003.

4
Karl Marx, *Capital*, Vol.1 1867.

5
Walter Benjamin, 'The Critique of Violence' in *Reflections* (Ed) Peter Demetz, Shocken, New York, 1986.

6
Tiziana Terranova, 'Free Labor: Producing Culture for the Digital Economy', 2000. Available at http://www.electronicbookreview.com/thread/techno-capitalism/voluntary

7
Mario Tronti, *La Politica al Tramonto*, Einaudi, Rome, 1998. With many thanks to Brett Neilson for the pointer and translation.

8
Silvia Federici, *Caliban and the Witch: Women, the Body and Primitive Accumulation*, Autonomedia, New York, 2004.

9
Freddy Scharmen, '"You must be logged in to do that!" - Myspace and Control' May, 2006. http://www.sevensix-five.net/myspace/myspacetwopointoh.html

10
Johan Söderberg, 'Reluctant Revolutionaries: The False Modesty of Reformist Critics of Copyright', 2004. http://info.interactivist.net/article.pl?sid=04/09/29/1411223

11
Richard Barbrook, 'The Hi-Tech Gift Economy', 1998. http://www.firstmonday.dk/issues/issue3_12/barbrook/

12
Henry Jenkins, 'Taking the You Out of YouTube?', 2006. http://www.henryjenkins.org/2006/11/googtube_tv_20_or_bubble_20.html

13
Werner Hamacher, 'Working Through Working', 1996. *Modernism/modernity* Volume 3, Number 1, January 1996, The Johns Hopkins University Press, pp. 23-56.

14
Andrew Feenberg, 'Democratic Rationalization: Technology, Power, and Freedom', 1992. http://dogma.free.fr/txt/AF_democratic-rationaliza-tion.htm

15
John McMurria, 'The YouTube Community', 2006. http://jot.communication.utexas.edu/flow/?jot=view&id=1995

16
Theodor Adorno & Max Horkheimer, *Dialectic of Enlightenment*, (Trans) John Cumming, Herder and Herder, New York, 1972.

17
For a discussion of the undercommons, see Fred Moten and Stefano Harney's 'The University and the Undercommons', *Social Text*, Issue 79, Duke University Press, 2004. Available at http://info.interactivist.net/article.pl?sid=05/04/23/1535258&mode=nested&tid=8

18
Jacques Derrida, *Mal d'Archive*, Galilée, Paris, 1995.

Angela Mitropoulos
<s0metim3s@optusnet.com.au> lives in Melbourne, Australia

Web 2.0 relies heavily on identikit forms of self-representation and sociability. Parallel to the 'authentic', self-promoting personae of MySpace, multi-user virtual worlds such as Second Life (SL) appear to offer a more malleable, playful version of life online. But as the imperatives of commercial exchange penetrate deeper into the networked imagination, is the gap between RL and VR what it used to be? Giorgio Agostoni reverse engineers material from across the net to construct a fictional readymade suspended between self-reinvention and self-management

THE LONG TALE
by Giorgio Agostoni

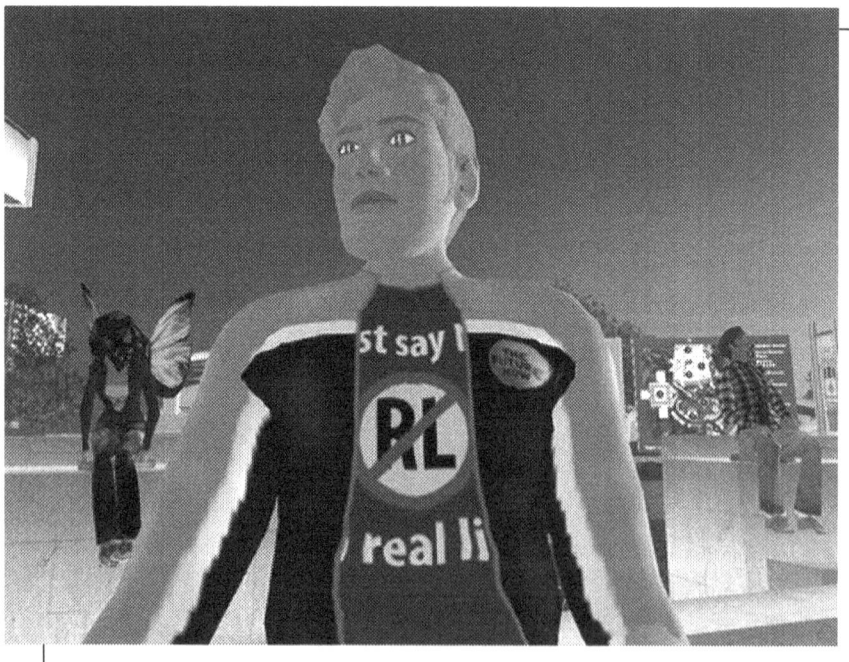

All images from Howard Rheingold's presentation in Second Life 'Participatory Media And The Pedagogy Of Civic Participation – The Transformation Of Education And Democracy', Autumn 2006, http://www.masternewmedia.org/news/2006/11/14/participatory_media_and_the_pedagogy.htm

1 Research

Robert Helmerich <helmerich88@...> wrote:

>I have recently been gathering material for an
>article that attempts to chart some of the
>projections and influences of science fiction
>upon current MMO platforms like *Second Life*. My
>aim is to determine if the abstraction of IT
>fetishes, and divergent visions of personal
>identity can be seen as a sign that a kind of
>technological schizophrenia is reconstituting the
>boundaries of daily life in the framework of a
>complex evolutionary context.
>
>Having now posted in several online groups
>concerned with technology, RP and fiction, I
>have been taken aback by the scope and depth of
>the speculation. As an outsider, I sometimes
>have great difficulty penetrating the tight,
>shifting fabric of unique signs, associations
>and coded images that arise within groups with
>private languages.

Any opinions are only as good as the biases that
form them. If you're new to this group then you
won't even know what those biases are likely to be
for any of us. I may rave about the character
designs, but deep down, perhaps it's just that I'm
a sucker for cute sullen girls in furry costumes.
But my review wouldn't tell you *that*.

As a bibliophile, the intertextuality of the
series may be jerk-off material for weeks. To
someone else, it may be pretentious name-dropping;
a shallow attempt to lend some credibility to an
otherwise weak plot-line. Then again, maybe we just
like to haze newcomers, in our own elitist way.

>I was wondering if any of you would be available
>and willing to comment on the series in relation
>to my research?
>(outlined above).
>
>Thanks in advance for your replies.
>
>Robert

The series draws from some very esoteric references: John C. Lilly is not very well known outside of certain circles; neither are Ted Nelson, Vannevar Bush, Cordwainer Smith or Tim Berners-Lee. VR, while a cultural staple, is still a technology covered by Clarke's Third Law. And the idea of virtuality overlapping deep reality is still a fantasy to most of the world.

Hope this helps. Have a look at the abridged archive too.

seawebb

2
∎

Morgana Aubret Sep 23rd 2006
permalink

I have a number of alts, some of which are unverified. In some ways they express different facets of my personality. In other ways, they are a method of dealing with the inadequacies of SL – lack of privacy, need for them to make groups and test permissions, backup repositories in case the asset server freaks out, etc.

In real life, most people do have multiple identities. The way they behave in front of their mother is different than the way they behave with their buddies at the bar is different from the way they behave at work. SL just makes it a lot easier to separate that out. Is that a good or a bad thing? In a world where you literally have no privacy – when anyone can contact you at any point via IM unless you are in busy mode – it is an essential thing.

Morgana is my good girl. She's the nice, polite, helpful businesswoman who is always ready to lend a hand. She tries hard never to be unduly cross with people, never to tell someone they have to figure out the rest on their own, and never to let anyone down. For someone who is highly introverted and antisocial IRL, it's impossible to be her all the time. I have to be able to not respond to the flood of people wanting my attention sometimes.

The downside is that people can use alts to game their friends and enemies. I don't. No one knows all of my alts except me, but when people do know my alts to any depth, I tend to reveal to them that they are my alts. I'm not interested in mind games. As for trusting others, I'm not a terribly trusting person IRL, although it is nice not standing next to some random person in line and not having to worry that they are the neighbor who secretly hates you. I find most people who have alts ISL tend to end up revealing them sooner or later. Little things give people away.

I have spoken on the phone and met SLers IRL. None of my alts do anything I wouldn't do. Would I disappear if all mine were revealed? Nope. Would I have a brand new alt immediately? Yep. (And I wonder how they would actually find all these links between multiple payment methods, multiple people in my household, and multiple computers used. How would they know who was whose?)

One thing I find very interesting is speculating about revealing the links from alts to mains. But what defines the 'main'? Is my 'main' my original SL account, the one with the biggest friend list, the one with the biggest 'name' ISL, the one that makes the most money? (All Morgana for me.) Is my main the one I prefer to be, the one most like me IRL, and the one I tend to reserve for my closest friends? (Not Morgana for me.) Is it the one in which I spend the most time? (Which tends to shift over time.) How would you define it?

Kristian Ming Sep 25th 2006
permalink
I admit my alts to LL because I don't want them coming back and punishing me for whatever

reason down the road. It also gives me pause, because I will stop and ask myself if I really want the Avatar or is it just an opportunity to get a clever name.

Most of my Avs are for Roleplay, and not in the Fur/Age/BDSM sense. I've got my Anime CatGrrl, my 'Tyler Durden', and numerous others.

One thing I will say, it's awfully nice to have some genderbent avs, because the selection of stuff for male avatars STINKS compared to women. My Blog

Karl Herber Sep 27th 2006
permalink
I agree about the hair for men sucking. Really short hair for men is next to impossible to find, and tends to come as part of a skin. Now I'm VERY happy with my skin, it's a good photorealistic one, and I'm not keen to change that for a lesser-quality skin just for the sake of a crew-cut hairstyle.

Curiously, a female friend of mine who plays SL and other MMORPGs always creates male characters instead of female ones, and told me it was because she got tired of being chatted up and propositioned for sex all the time.

3
---

abandonedstudio
Current mood:: pensive
Posted:: May 26 2006 15:15
Subject:: Origins

WARNING: SPOILERS BELOW

The story begins at Tachibana Labs, where the enterprising scientist Eiri Masami is working on an innovative internet protocol. This IP (IPv7) is closely patterned after Ted Nelson's Xanadu system, and is designed to be the ultimate method of accessing and sharing information across the Net.

While this is Tachibana Lab's intention, Eiri Masami believes that Protocol 7 will allow humans to connect to the Net without devices. If we enter the Net without devices, we can potentially lose our sense of self. Good or bad, total connectedness also implies total loss of ego and identity.

Having studied the data on the KIDS project (aka the Kensington Experiment) and on the Schumann Resonance, Eiri goes on to secretly embed code into Tachibana Lab's latest internet protocol (IPv7) thus allowing device-less mass communications.

The effect of Eiri's code in IPv7 is to transform the collective unconscious (as described by Jung) into collective consciousness. It is interesting that in the story, Tachibana Labs 'succeeded in analysing the molecular structure of the human genome' (layer 11 'INFORNOGRAPHY'). That Tachibana Labs were able to do this may have provided the means for Eiri to create IPv7.

When Tachibana Labs discover that Eiri has embedded device-less protocols into their software, they terminate his employment, as there would

maybe we just like to haze newcomers in our own elitist way

be no business or market for their products in a world with device-less mass communications. Eiri, however, has mastered the ability to communicate within the collective unconscious, and commits suicide, believing that he is the first to evolve into a deus ex machina, and plans to recruit other humans to join him.

Perhaps out of greed, or perhaps out of guilt for unleashing Eiri's protocols into the Net, Tachibana Labs create a daring counter-measure to combat this influence. This counter-measure is Rein. A sophisticated bio-organism or 'homunculus by artificial ribosome' which can interact in the 'real world' as a human being. She is created as a middle-school girl and the Iwakura family is assigned to 'raise' her.

It is Tachibana's hope that through Rein, Eiri's code can be overwritten. Their feeling is that if software can learn the importance of existence on a material plane, people will be prevented from following Eiri into the Net. Later, when Eiri confronts Rein, he tries to convince her that he is her creator in a ploy to enlist her to his side.
Randell Lawrence
15:15 PM | 0 Comments | 0 Kudos | Add Comment

Wolfie
Posted:: May 26 2006 17:34
Subject:: Re: Origins

Nice interpretation Randell

It can be argued that Rein is deterring people form reaching both extremes (real and virtual), but I don't think Tachibana Labs could've done that. They didn't know Rein's specifications, they just sensed that she was different. Something's amiss.

I still believe that Rein came from elsewhere... Tachibana Labs were more interested in her than they were knowledgeable about her. But indeed a good teaser interpretation. More should be pondered on Rein's identity and origin.
Wolfie Toutoumouchan
17:34 PM | 0 Comments | 0 Kudos | Add Comment

Grego
Posted:: May 27 2006 13:01
Subject:: Re: Origins

Show quoted text
That is an interesting idea – the real world as virtual memory.

So that's why it sucks that much... it's never been defragmented!

We took care of that with the upload of Reality 2.0, but it looks as if the file system drivers need some work.
13:01 PM | 0 Comments | 0 Kudos | Add Comment

James London
Posted:: May 28 2006 13:22
Subject:: Re: Origins

Would you shed your body for life on the Net?
13:22 PM | 0 Comments | 0 Kudos | Add Comment

Arakume
Posted:: May 28 2006 14:27
Subject:: Re: Origins

I'd settle for one that wouldn't change neurosis mid-life. Granted, moving is traumatic for everyone. But if I can't get away from the noise and the constant demands for cuddles and attention, why shouldn't I?
-Arakume-
14:27 PM | 0 Comments | 0 Kudos | Add Comment

jinxie
Posted:: May 28 2006 14:52
Subject:: Re: Origins
On this topic: My VP of technology gave me an

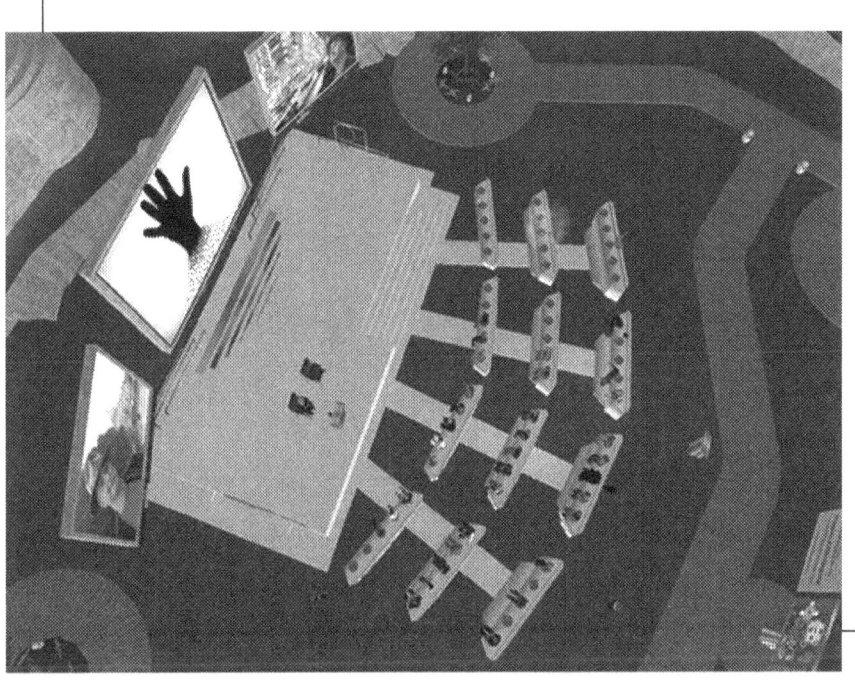

article to read from Business Week the other day – about Second Life. The massively multiplayer world, geared towards individual creativity. All content in the world is created by users – not game developers.

After letting my City of Tedium account expire, I decided to give it a try, drawn mostly by the $9.99 one-time subscription and free client download... well, I've been known to spend more on less. It sounded intriguing, perhaps the closest thing yet to Neal Stephenson's 'Metaverse', a place to just hang out in the shape of an av, meet new people, and even conduct business. This is a very short recap of my first impressions, as I've just finished the tutorial, created a character, and wandered around a little.

In Second Life, I am Mika Sismondi (after Rein's sister, – the one who goes crazy). I have yet to pay any money to the SL folk but I'm starting to have lots of fun there. I bought a nice outfit, which took me a while to figure out how to get out of the box. I've teleported all over the place, and trespassed dozens of people's

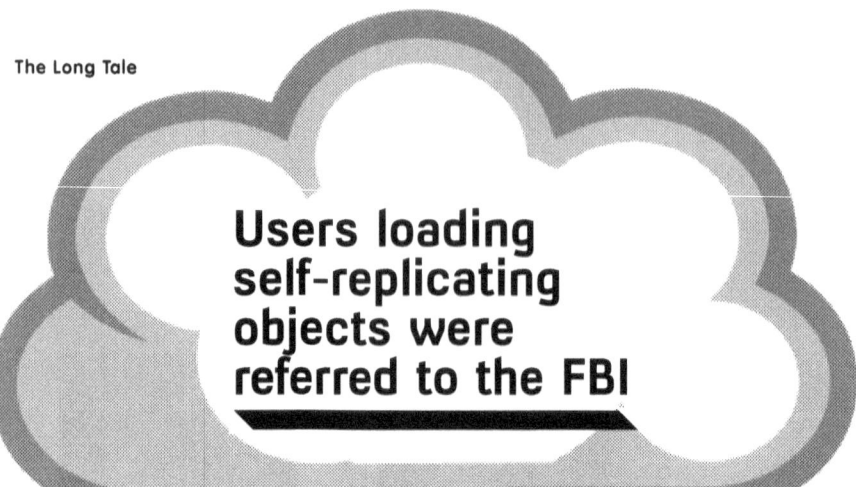

Users loading self-replicating objects were referred to the FBI

personal homes, looking at all their stuff.

It's always a little surprising to non-gamers that people would spend so much time doing virtual things. SL estimates that the programmer time required to build the world that exists there now would cost something like a billion dollars, if you paid for it. While this seems kind of bizarre, to me sports is the same thing. I just don't get sports. I have never been able to understand how people can spend so much time and money on a totally unproductive activity – watching sports. MMO worlds are not any crazier to me.

I was thinking I might play around with it occasionally. I don't know where I would find the time? Between blogging, working, taking care of various life needs, and studying – where could I find time for SL? I was thinking thought that it would be fun to build a house where CR

people could meet as avatars. Perhaps we could exchange recipes? Sit and chat? Maybe we can make fake food and pretend to eat it.

14:52 PM | 0 Comments | 0 Kudos | Add Comment

Wolfie
Posted:: May 28 2006 15:11
Subject:: Re: Origins

Talk about shedding your mortal coil for life on the Net… Have a look at the article below... :- Wolfie Toutoumouchan

POST-MORTEM SOCIAL NETWORKS
By FRANCESCA M. MARI
The Harvard Crimson Magazine
Wednesday, May 01, 2006

Unlike Facebook.com, MySpace.com does not delete profiles of the deceased. In fact, another site called MyDeathSpace.com exists solely to catalog them.

Launched in December of 2005, MyDeathSpace.com displays a

MySpace.com user's cause of death and any related news articles alongside a picture of the deceased linked to their MySpace.com profile.

Because MySpace.com is most popular amongst people college-aged and younger, the deaths are usually tragic (suicides, automobile accidents, and murders) or completely abnormal (a kid killed by a rare cancer, two teens found dead with their heads inside an 8-foot helium balloon).

According to the site's founder, Mike Patterson, there are more than a thousand deceased listed. 'It's supposed to be an eye opening experience,' Patterson says. 'You're supposed to be shocked by what you see.'

The site, he adds, receives about 20,000 unique visitors a day, and each visitor clicks on average between 10 and 15 times.

In his spare hours, Patterson enters into the site the new deaths, 99 percent of which he says are submitted to him through his website.

'It just seems that's where everything in life is going—online,' Patterson says. 'If a friend dies, you're not going to be able to go to the cemetery and leave flowers for him or her. It's a lot easier to do it online, whether it be going to their MySpace account and leaving comments or creating a memorial profile.'

When asked about Facebook.com's policy to delete profiles of the deceased, Patterson says, 'The friends of the deceased obviously want the deceased person's profile up so they can remember them and leave comments on the profile to mourn them. I'd be pissed if my friend died and didn't have a MySpace profile. I'd be kind of sad.'

15:11 PM | 0 Comments | 0 Kudos | Add Comment

4 Self-replicating objects

When the first self-replication attacks occurred, the contingency was to incorporate code to turn off simulators (sims, the 256x256m segments of land which make up the grid) in order to stunt the growth of the attacks. This countermeasure helped contain the outburst of the virus, much like amputating a foot to save the leg. But the real weakness lies in the underlying model that has informed the architecture from the beginning, which is based on valuing real-estate as the sole element of the world that is metered and charged for. This has had a curious effect – it means that the world does not naturally charge users for processor usage and storage space, and means that a self-replicating script is hard to detect. To fully address this problem, assets would need a strong sense of ownership and would need to be charged for, like real estate. This would make scripts naturally accountable.

However it wasn't until more recently that the 'Grey Goo Fence' was incorporated, which uses a formula to decide how many objects and how often they can be 'rezzed' (loaded into the world) by a resident on a per sim basis. This should manage to stunt the lightning-speed spread and allow more time to react to an outburst. But as the defenses become more elaborate, so do the weapons, and there are now more distributed attacks which send the self-replicating objects to other users. Upon receiving these objects, they lie dormant in the residents inventory and only if the resident chooses to rez this object can it continue its spread. The defense for this at present is an attempt to educate residents not to accept objects from people they don't know.

In a worst case scenario, self-replicating objects will get you banned. Usually because they can bring down simulators and/or harass other players. Self-replicating objects that are an annoyance of any fashion are against community standards. So far, every noticeable case of uncontrolled or excessive self-replicating objects has resulted in threats of banishment. Except in the latest instance where the users were referred to the F.B.I.

5 Hardware

From: 'abc def' <donuselinux@...>
Posted: Wed Jan 9, 2006 6:43 pm
Subject: NAVI

Show quoted text

I don't remember anything sexy about Rein (except perhaps when she stripped down to her camisole to avoid static when she worked on her system, which I found attractive). I don't know, I really liked the bear-suit she often wore. It seems like years ago now that someone wandered through here, wondering just what she was wearing UNDER the bear-suit...

Reply | Forward

From: DRAGON W <dragonstar3014@...>
Posted: Wed Jan 9, 2006 7:07 pm
Subject: Re: NAVI

Note: Mr.Konaka wrote three Rein characters:

1) Childish "Rein" (The Rein we first see)
2) Advanced "Rein" in the Net (The Jungian Shadow or Freudian Id)
3) Evil "Rein" in his scenario (Her 2nd half in a split persona)

Consequentially, Rein's bear pyjamas would be a winning shot to impress some fans who enthuse over nymph-like characters. This particular novelty may be important in the genre.

(Rein's cross-hair detainment was Mr.Abe's idea, but the producer decided the asymmetrical hair-style for Rein.)

> Konaka:
> The bear pyjamas are Mr.Kishida's idea. The bear pyjamas in my works were so abundant that I opposed them at first. Mr. Kishida didn't say why he made Rein wear the bear pyjamas. However, Supervisor Nakamura said "Kissy (Mr.Kishida's pet) always wore sunglasses." So, I understood that it is like a shield for Rein. Finally, she wore the bear pyjamas when she cocoons from the outer environment and when she talked with family.

Reply | Forward

From: Ilya V. Vasilef <Ilyavv4evr@...>
Posted: Wed Jan 10, 2006 6:13 pm
Subject: Re: NAVI

What do you guys think, or have you already talked about something like this perhaps?
Basically as far as I could tell, all NAVI's have clustering ability built-in, and it looked like Rein's local network connections were getting faster (to the point of being practically sci-fi) and she was adding more computers all the time.

I noticed that the connections evolved very quickly from thin cable (probably something like thinnet or Cat-V) to much larger cables, probably

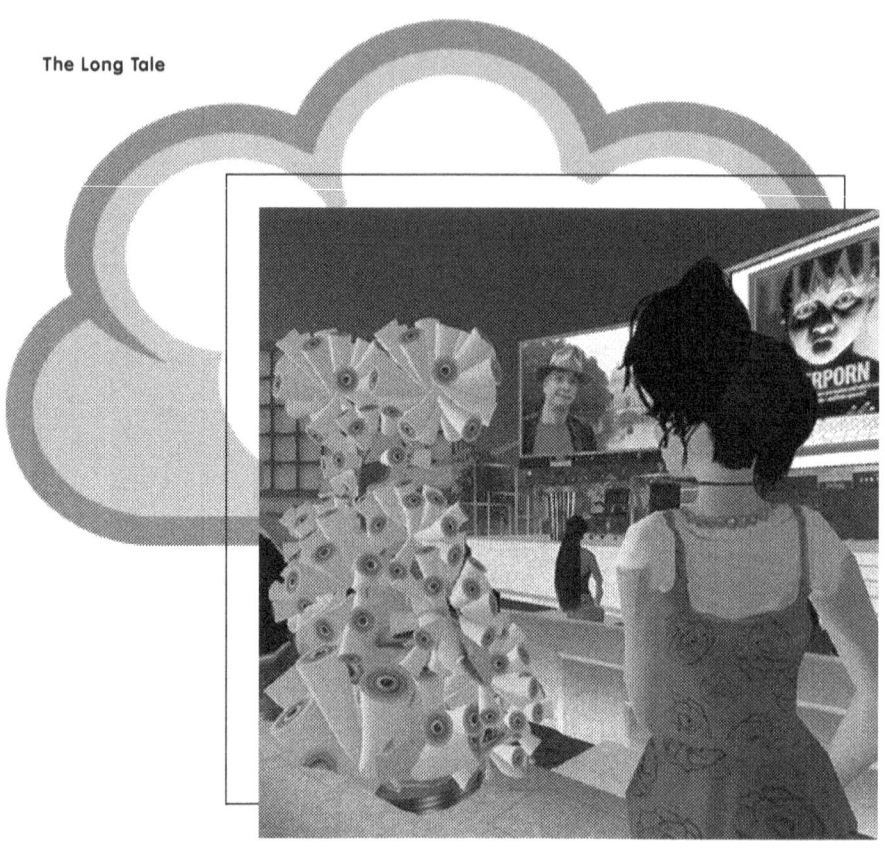

something similar to FEC with Cat-V bundles.

Rein was probably over-clocking some of those machines too, given the insane cooling systems needed. I think it was in layer three where the motherboard was glowing due to the clock speed... no wonder she went full immersion cooling. <grin> she might be using the experimental Cat 7 cable; The same size as regular Ethernet cable, but can do some insane speeds of 7 or 8 gigs per second. I just always assume that SE takes place in another 5 years, because I don't think any over clocker today would be able to get enough processors going at any speed to need carbon cooling. Maybe it was Inert Fluorocarbon cooling (Fluorinert TM?) I recall one documented over-clocking experiment which used just this... they were using a heat exchanger bathed in liquid nitrogen.

Reply | Forward

From: Wendigo (107 Porn Bots Tagged & Bagged)
<wendigo@...>
Posted: Wed Jan 10, 2006 10:55 pm
Subject: Re: NAVI

Yah, by the end it seemed like there was so much
condensation water that she was running a steam
powered computer! I'd definitely have to agree
with you. One thing that always got me was how
Rein's computer system gets bigger and bigger. It
reminds me of my own system, how first it was only
just the monitor and cpu. Then comes the printer,
scanner and cable modem. Then the web-cam and mic,
and later on the joystick and external disk.
Reply | Forward

From: Arakume <arakumechan@...>
Posted: Wed Jan 11, 2006 01:06 am
Subject: Re: NAVI

my liitle nihonshu ippai, wouldn't it more
straight forward and effective to move ourselves
into the abstract realm to be with what we want?

<dreamy>

If only I were more clever. Just as soon as I kick
the shoes off and let my hair down, something
unwanted comes crashing through.

<brow furrows>

Perhaps a taller fence is in order.
-Arakume-
Reply | Forward

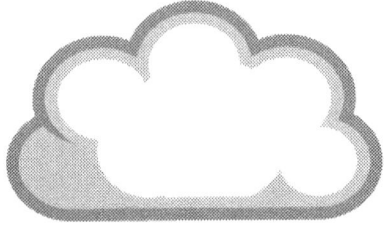

Giorgio Agostoni <g.agostoni@gmail.com>
is an artist. He makes disjointed texts
and readymades

SWARM FORMS: ON PLATFORMS AND CREATIVITY
by Olga Goriunova

Will the 'hive mind' of social networking replace classical forms of knowledge production? Comparing Web 2.0 and small-scale, self-run cultural platforms, Olga Goriunova maintains the possibility for originality in both contexts, while identifying how the same old commercial and institutional pressures still operate

The term 'platform' is so common today it makes people sick (though not as much as 'Web 2.0' does). It is thought to have originated with Tim O'Reilly and his article on Web 2.0 in which he describes 'the web as platform', not as a figure of speech but a description of concrete developments.[1] Back in 2002, when I started conceiving of my work on the software art repository Runme.org in terms of a platform on which to build an art trend, it was difficult to decide on which term to apply. 'Platform' only had a history of metaphorical usage, such as with the Dutch 'Virtueel Platform' which

The term 'platform' is so common today it makes people sick

was established in 1998 as an expertise centre 'stimulating innovation and supporting e-culture'.[2]

It seems that the web as 'platform' in O'Reilly's terms bears a mainly technical meaning. A platform spans 'all connected devices', 'delivering software as a continually-updated service'; 'a platform for interacting with content'.[3] Even 'the web and all its connected devices as one global platform' implies the meaning of a platform as of a *server* (or servers) 'delivering desktop-like applications over the web'.[4] Thus, a platform for Web 2.0 adepts serves applications to end-users through a web browser allowing interaction with content. Such a definition is useful and helps make a distinction for designers and programmers between Web 1.0 that supposedly was about static html-based web sites (with CGI or Perl on the back-end) and Web 2.0's dynamic platforms generally built with 'CSS for layout, XML for data, XHTML for markup, JavaScript and the DOM for behavior...' on the front end and 'PHP or (especially) Ruby on Rails' on the back-end.[5]

However, this description does not adequately address the politics of the technical architectures and applications involved. O'Reilly and his followers try to do this by nodding towards the fostering of community, collaboration, the 'architecture of participation', 'rich-user experiences', and 'collective intelligence', but continuously fail to prove that such cultural phenomena were not present in the times of what they term Web 1.0. My criticism is not original; Slate.com has been calling Web 2.0 a technical upgrade, while the participatory or social aspects of Web 2.0 are 'what the Web was supposed to be all along', as Tim Berners-Lee puts it.[6]

'Art platform' was the term I came up with as a solution for what to call an online platform that enables the building of a cultural movement entirely through the use of its own mechanisms. It describes a web platform that solicits, induces and produces a cultural or artistic phenomenon. Examples of such platforms include Micromusic.net, an 8-bit music platform, Runme.org, a software art repository, and Udaff.com, a 'mate lit' platform (mate or mat lit is my term for a current literary genre deploying obscene, colloquial, orthographic Russian discourse).[7] Two years ago, trying to provide a definition of an art platform, I wrote:

> A platform differentiates itself from other websites by the relations of creative, social, instrumental, educational and historical character it establishes and is involved into. A platform is aimed at supporting and

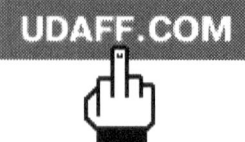

runme.org - say it with software art!

stimulating creative initiatives and work, and it provides a possibility for continuous exhibition of the artefacts, often accompanied by reactions to them, various discussions. Sometimes there is also a set of instruments for particular kind of creative work available. A platform often also puts efforts into translating digital creative processes into offline and more official cultural scenes, establishing connections between cultural movements of different times and orders. Most platforms organize (ir)regular 'real-life' gatherings such as festivals, concerts, workshops or those of a less formal nature.[8]

Most parts of this description can be applied today to blogging, photo-sharing and other platforms. However, the art platforms I refer to are all quite classical static web sites. And, on top of building 'communities', 'experiences' and 'collective knowledge', they build distinctive cultural products, whether regarded as digital folk, creative practices of everyday or artistic trends.

An art platform appears as a reaction to the development of a particular cultural creative practice it focuses on. It is quickly built by a few enthusiasts. A platform is administered , and all incoming projects moderated by, a small group of people (usually 1-5). It has an open database with a user-friendly interface anyone can download from/upload to. It accumulates a number of creative products that in turn attract new users and new products. Building a database of works, a platform chooses a particular mechanism of reward and distinction, be it voting or featuring, and contributes to the discourse and context of the practice it works within. Working with the 'grey' zones of cultural production, with grass-root practices, such platforms can create significant artistic and cultural phenomena, and transfer the practice onto a different cultural level.

If we look at the interface, art platforms can be clearly differentiated from blogs. Art platforms are single interface platforms, and blogs or tagging platforms are multiple interface platforms. Single interface platforms have a single entrance, a point of concentration, of maximum understanding of the resource. Such an interface may include a list of categories, whether a straightforward taxonomic database interface, as in the case of Runme.org, or of the latest texts, as with Udaff.com. If you visit a multiple interface platform there is no home page or main entrance. In the blogosphere, you navigate through personal blogs, through photographs and cross-references, by means of user names, friends, comments and links. Although banal, this distinction reveals a further, more fundamental one: single interface platforms are devoted to a single 'theme', a shared aesthetic, creative, even political horizon.

If on multiple interface platforms there are tools that help maintain the 'healthy' functioning of the system (for instance, 'abuse teams' in the case of blogs), with single interface platforms there is a need for moderators who are responsible for the development of the interface, which in fact means control over the content development of the entire system.

Such centralisation renders moderation very crucial, and is far from being 'automated curation'.[9] It is a taste-

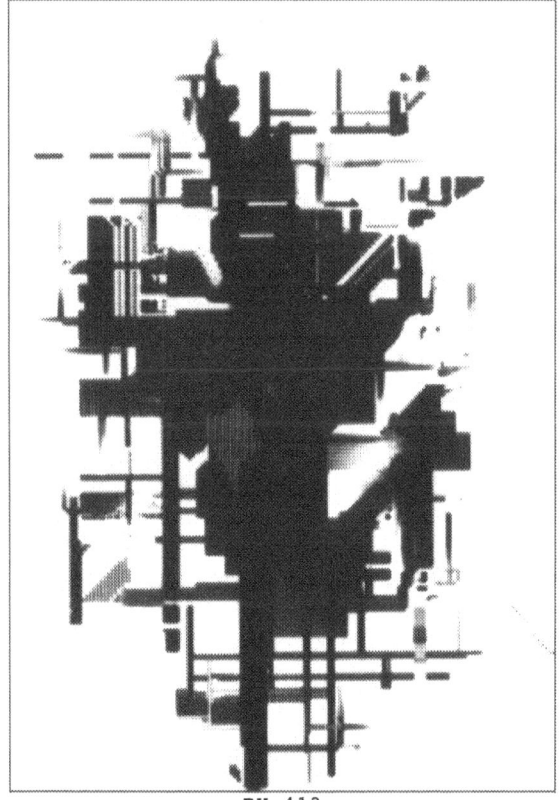
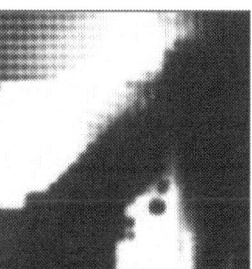
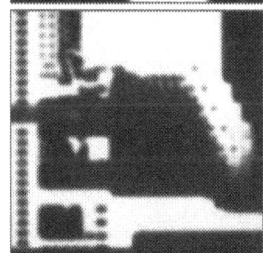
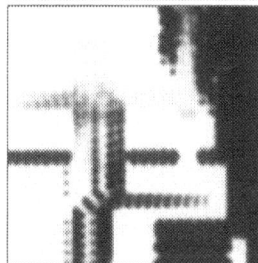

BX-413

Image: Ant Scott, Glitch Art, *BX-413*, 2005,
http://www.runme.org/project/+GlitchArt/

based, individualised decision-making process developed over time. Precise moderation, especially at the beginning, and the considered construction of a system is necessary to the survival of the platform and success of the trend. Moderation, together with users' input, helps develop the cultural movement and its discourse.

Multiple interface platforms users visit selected pages. With singular

giving it a theoretical, social or political dimension.

However, I would like to add that in terms of how and what they (can) potentially produce, art platforms and other platforms are not so different and can complement each other. This possibility exists against a general climate of mistrust on the part of researchers and intellectuals over the quality of the knowledge produced on platforms. There

single interface platforms	multiple interface platforms
navigate through taxonomy (common staircase)	navigate through personal pages, comments, links
common theme, construction of cultural trend	common type of activity
administration: control over the development of entire system	administration: maintaining the over-all healthy functioning
administrator: curator	administrator: police
visitor: researching the entire resource/ researching a cultural movement	visitor: researching individual pages, opinions, results of creative activities
user: developing an artistic movement	user: optimising personal life, partici-pating, creating, expressing

interface platforms, the user, interested in the trend the platform is devoted to, can explore almost the entire database. Contributing to such a platform, the user enters and co-creates a content rich context. With such platforms it is possible to develop an artistic movement, to add some missing elements to a creative activity,

is a continuous outcry on the part of some theorists and developers, claiming that the horizontalisation of knowledge and power celebrated by projects such as Wikipedia is dangerous. Jaron Lanier talks of the dangers of online collectivism and the belief in the wisdom of the collective. Larry Sanger criticises not specifically the celebration of amateurism but attacks on professionalism and expertise. Jürgen Habermas claims the use of the internet weakens the position of the traditional intellectual and undermines the achievements of the public sphere.[10]

However, the institution and construction of knowledge on Wikipedia, for instance, is really no different to the construction of offline encyclopedias. According to Wikipedia etiquette, as Fernanda Vegas and Martin Wattenberg mention in their study, before posting to an article it is desirable to discuss the prepared text on an article's 'talk page' with others, including 'permanent editors' of the article.[11] Trust for a certain author is built on the 'reputation' she develops over her history of participation in Wikipedia, and most authors possess individual personae known to others. The history of changes of an article presents a quite detailed and documented 'history of argument' and disagreement over a subject fighting its way through. The roles of institutions participating in the invention and construction of knowledge offline, such as scientific magazines with their peer-reviews or publishing houses with their publications and conferences, are seriously transformed but to a large degree reproduced online.

Wikipedia is a unique example, however. It should not serve as the face of Web 2.0 or some new generation of 'dangers'. Nor should it be mixed with tagging, blogging or mapping platforms which are much more oriented toward individual than collective production. The central claim here is that, contra the critics of social network-based knowledge, the creativity of users across all kinds of platforms, from digital folklore, creative and liberating practices of everyday life, subcultural expressivity, and graphorrhea to artistic production, is capable of producing 'original' results, especially if certain human-technical decisions help channel the process.

For instance, with art platforms, the technical bottlenecks of moderating, featuring, voting and making comments that channel the collective effort help create an artistic or cultural phenomenon. An art platform works as an art institution – it allows for the bias of the curator or editor; it allows for the storage and exhibition of works, as do museums or libraries with journals; it allows for contextualising, as do publications or conferences; it allows for feedback and peer review, as do magazines. An art platform produces histories, identities, knowledge and social clusters, exactly in the manner of those interrelations constituting power which Foucault grasped. It represents a quite centred power model that is seemingly not characteristic of platforms considered to be Web 2.0 services.

In order to create a focus, all platforms apply similar mechanisms rooted in the offline histories of power and institutions, however. For instance, when a community devoted to certain topics is formed on a blogging platform, a moderator turns up, a set of rules arises, and often after a while postings are re-filtered and organised in a database with a

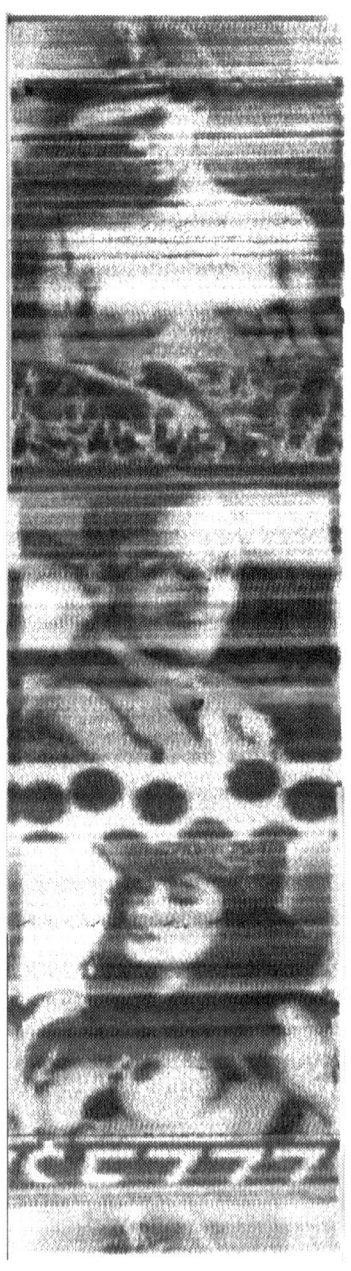

single interface platforms are devoted to a single 'theme', a shared aesthetic, creative, even political horizon

straightforward taxonomic interface. Such filters, human and technical, help re-create the figure of the professional or even intellectual, with individual judgement, taste and insight. It is a figure that re-vitalises the zombie of the traditional intellectual specialist, making it more 'autonomous' but also more vulnerable.

Bourdieu describes the intellectual as an historical product formed by a struggle between the forces of economics and politics, a struggle for autonomy.[12] The authority of intellectuals derives from their specific position in the relatively autonomous world of art or science and their adherence to values such as disinterestedness, ethical purity and expertise. Bourdieu calls for the preservation of the intellectual's autonomy currently endangered by corporate sponsorship of universities, and their direct subordination to business and political imperatives. Answering Lanier's criticism of Wikipedia, its co-founder, Larry Sanger, counters:

Image: Paul Slocum, *dot_matrix_synth*, 2003, http://runme.org/project/+dot-matrix-synth/

Slashdotters would not simply stand for a system in which some hand-selected group of editors choose or promote posts; but if the result is decided by an impersonal algorithm, then it's okay. It isn't that the Slashdotters have a rational belief that the cream will rise to the top, under the system; people use the system just because it seems *fairer or more equal* to them.[13]

While traditional bastions of knowledge/power suffer a crisis of authority arising from their loss of autonomy, many internet users, believing they are able to own their means of production, circulation and consecration, become the new intellectuals fighting for a 'fairer' space or principle, re-establishing autonomy through technical or human-technical decisions. They are in fact led by the very same imperatives Bourdieu describes.

Working on a platform is an economically vulnerable position. Such labour is usually performed by 'freaks' for free or for micro-money obtained for purposes loosely associated with their work on the platform. Nevertheless, a moderator or developer is well aware of their economic precariousness. The work of the ordinary user, by contrast, is not ordinarily understood as labour per se. It does, however, belong to the category of 'immaterial labour' as described by Italian marxists such as Maurizio

Lazzarato, Paolo Virno, Tiziana Terranova and others. Such cultural production provides new types of products and relations which alter the process of surplus value extraction; it drives innovation, trains in precariousness, locates social desires.

The means of cultural production, in this case platforms, necessarily belong to the capitalist class and are either bought by companies or – today – built by them from scratch. These companies not only want to control the technical means, but the data as well. However, platforms' licences and terms of use vary drastically. Some, like Tagzania, use a Creative Commons licence, but most platforms stipulate shared copyright with the content's author.

Tim O'Reilly, an originator of the idea of the '*user ownership of data*' (an oft repeated but rather unclear statement), claims:

> Much as the rise of proprietary software has led to the Free Software movement, we expect the rise of proprietary databases to result in a Free Data movement within the next decade.[14]

However, there are several issues worth raising concerning the user's data and its ownership. First, data is not that important to platform owners. What is important is the presence of users and the continuous use of the platform's facilities. For instance, one cannot easily gather all the postings to a personal blog

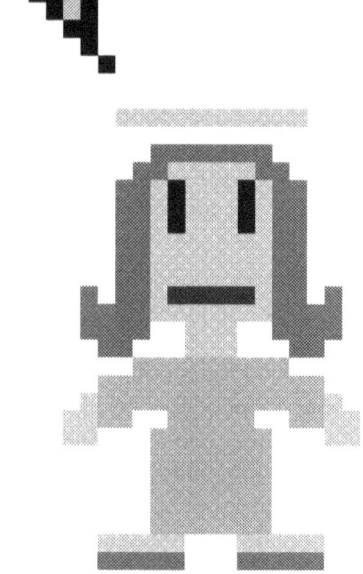

along with their commentaries and transfer that data to another platform. The data is intertwined in the platform and, until she loses interest, the user will be back to work on the relevant platform she has already devoted time to. Secondly, a person willing to make an open or free data platform will (and did) eventually find out that traffic volumes are too high for an individual to sustain and will eventually sell it. This complex set of interdependencies defines the current picture.

As Tiziana Terranova puts it:

> … this mode also signals the emergence of new machines of control and subjectification which reimpose hierarchical relations at the service of social reproduction and the production of surplus value. These are moments which turn qualitative, intensive differences into quantitative relations of exchange and equivalence; which enclose the open and dissipative potential of cultural production into differential hierarchies; which accumulate the rewards or work carried out by larger social assemblages…[15]

However, Wikipedia managed to choose a different economic model for itself. The vicious circle described above can only be challenged if platforms are considered public spaces, analogous to those of a city. This said, other problems linked to public space and coupled with the issues relating to the nature of networks will inevitably arise.

The situation is different with art platforms. If platforms are increasingly corporately owned, art platforms tend to be run by enthusiasts. The developer of a platform can sell it, the moderator of an art platform can't. An art platform's moderator is the one who registered the domain name, collaborated on or supervised the technical development of the resource, invested, along with other moderators, significant amounts of time into 'raising' a platform, deciding on almost every single aspect of its development.

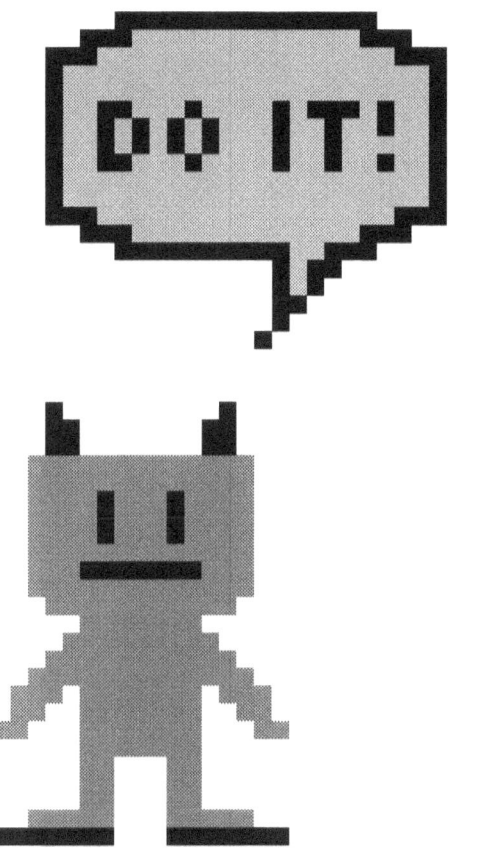

Olga Goriunova

The term 'Web 2.0' was created as a business slogan, a logo, so it came as little surprise to hear that O'Reilly had applied for a patent on Web 2.0 as a service mark in 2003. The patent was pending the whole time O'Reilly was promoting it as a generic term. Despites the term's poverty, its success subsumes all the attempts to talk about social software, a participatory web, collective creation and other, different and pre-existing models.

Like Meccano, many buildings can be constructed from the same constitutive elements, and different purposes and principles inform different platforms. If we understand them in this way, platforms cannot in general be stigmatised as loci of the unoriginal 'hive mind', and there is no need for a term like Web 2.0.

Footnotes

1
Tim O'Reilly, 'What Is Web 2.0. Design Patterns and Business Models for the Next Generation of Software', 2005
http://www.oreillynet.com/pub/a/oreilly/tim/news/2005/09/30/what-is-web-20.html

2
Virteel Platform, 'About', see:
http://www.virtueelplatform.nl/set-223-en.html

3
Andrew Orlowski, 'Web 2.0: It's ... like your brain on LSD!',
http://www.theregister.co.uk/2005/10/21/web_two_point_nought_poll/;
Richard MacManus & Joshua Porter, 'Web 2.0 for Designers', http://www.digital-web.com/articles/web_2_for_designers/

4
Dion Hinchcliffe, 'The State of Web 2.0',
http://web2.wsj2.com/the_state_of_web_20.htm; Paul Graham, 'Web 2.0',
http://www.paulgraham.com/web20.html#f1n

The moderator(s) and the users together create a cultural entity which is coherent, specific and, importantly, small-scale. Its subject is avant-garde and marginal.

Without moderation and the trust of its users, the art platform turns into a dead archive. This is the core principle by which it is distinguished from other platforms that largely run 'by themselves', demanding maintenance from the owner in a way comparable to the maintenance of a bicycle. In conclusion, it is rather unlikely that art platforms in their current shape will become economically appealing to companies.

Image: Eugenio Tisselli, *angel&devil*,
http://runme.org/project/+angeldevil/

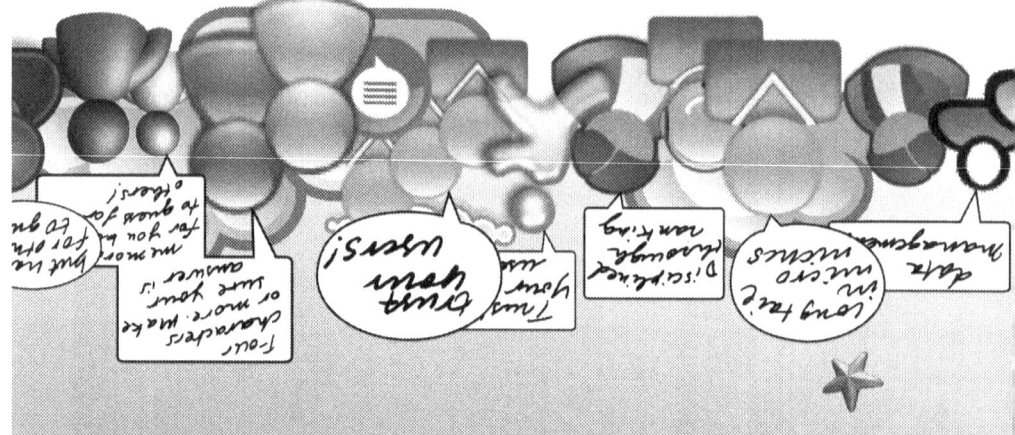

5

Jeffrey Zeldman, 'Web 3.0',
http://www.alistapart.com/articles/web3point0

6

Paul Boutin, 'Web 2.0 Doesn't Live Up to its Name',
http://www.slate.com/id/2138951/; Nate Anderson,
'Tim Berners-Lee on Web 2.0: "Nobody Knows What
it Means"',
http://arstechnica.com/news.ars/post/20060901-
7650.html

7

For a more detailed analysis of mate lit, see Olga
Goriunova, '"Male literature" of Udaff.com and Other
Networked Artistic Practices of the Cultural
Resistance', in *Control + Shift. Public and Private Usages
of the Russian Internet*, eds. Henrike Schmidt, Katy
Teubener, Natalja Konradova, Norderstedt: Books on
Demand, 2006.

8

Olga Goriunova & Alexei Shulgin, 'From Art on
Networks to Art on Platforms', in *Data Browser, volume
3: Curating Immateriality: On the Work of the Curator in
the Age of Network Systems*, ed. Joasia Krysa, New York:
Autonomedia, 2006.

9

The term 'automated curating' appears to originate from
Eva Grubinger's project *C@C – Computer-Aided
Curating* (1993-1995). For an account of the project, see
Eva Grubinger, 'C@C, Computer-Aided Curating
(1993-1995) Revisited', in Joasia Krysa, op. cit.

10

Jaron Lanier, 'Digital Maoism: The Hazards of the New
Online Collectivism', 2006,
http://www.edge.org/3rd_culture/lanier06/lanier06_ind
ex.html; Larry Sanger, 'Why Wikipedia Must Jettison
Its Anti-Elitism', 2004,
http://www.kuro5hin.org/story/2004/12/30/142458/25;
Jürgen Habermas, 'Towards a United States of Europe',
2006, http://www.signandsight.com/features/676.html

11

Fernanda Vegas, Martin Wattenberg, Kushal Dave,
'Studying Cooperation and Conflict between Authors
with *history flow* Visualisations', 2004,
http://alumni.media.mit.edu/~fviegas/papers/history_fl
ow.pdf

12

Pierre Bourdieu, *The Rules of Art*, Cambridge: Polity
Press, 2005

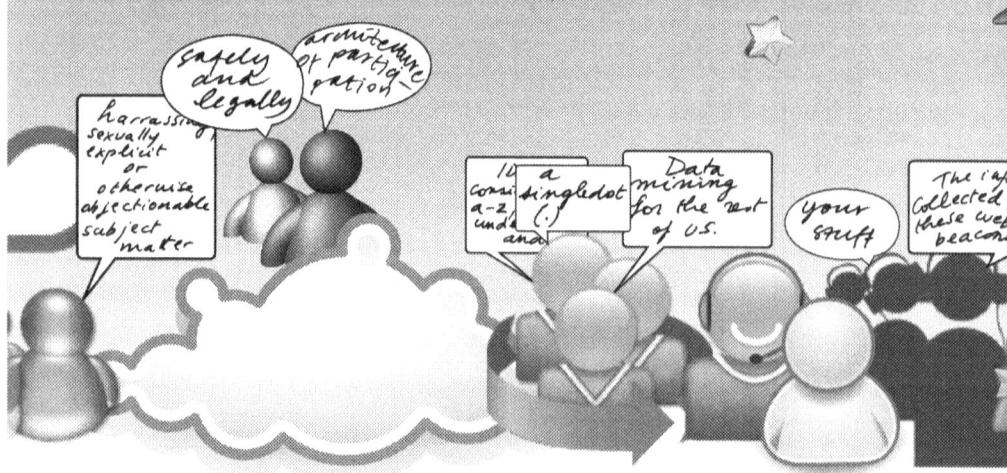

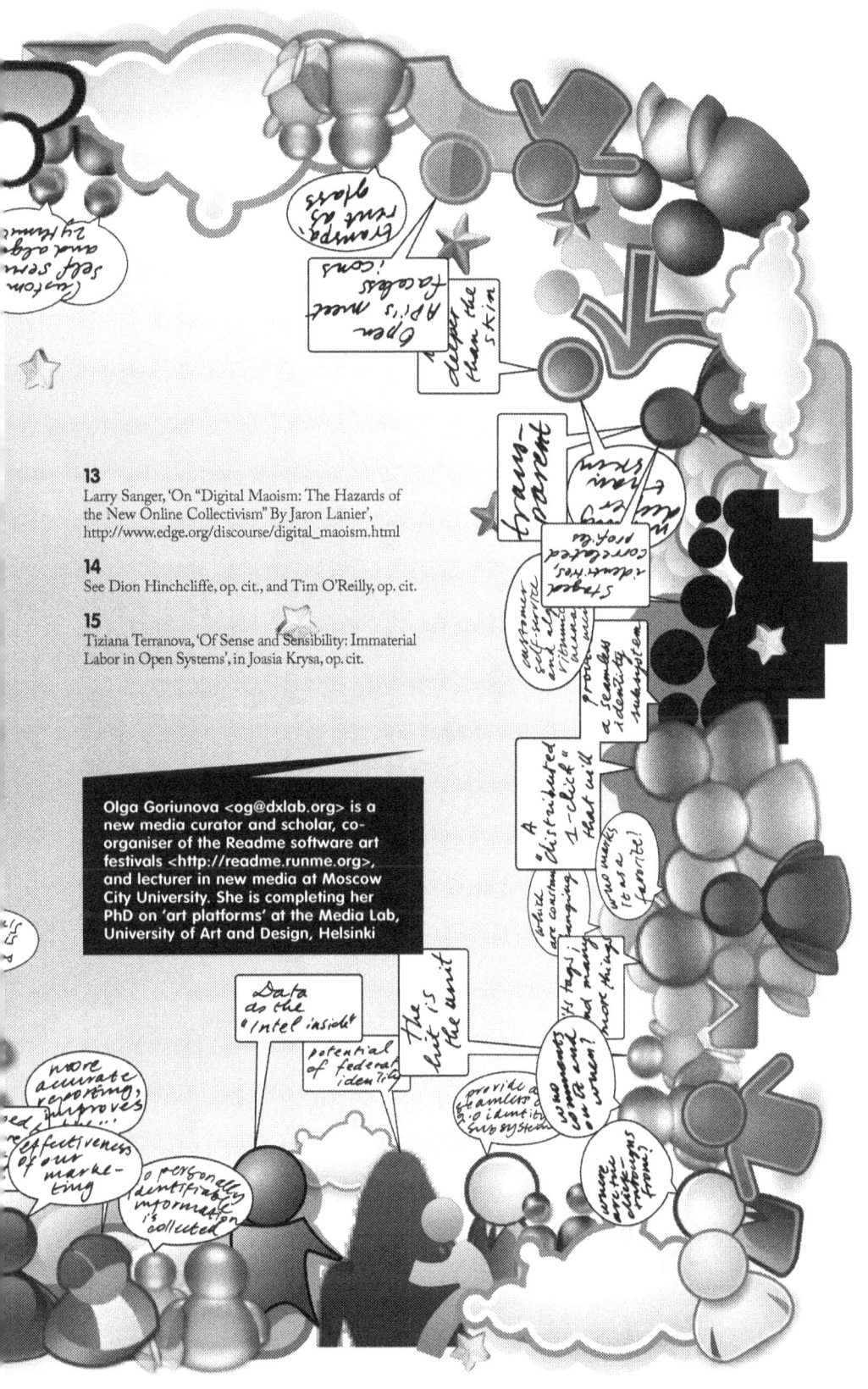

13
Larry Sanger, 'On "Digital Maoism: The Hazards of the New Online Collectivism" By Jaron Lanier', http://www.edge.org/discourse/digital_maoism.html

14
See Dion Hinchcliffe, op. cit., and Tim O'Reilly, op. cit.

15
Tiziana Terranova, 'Of Sense and Sensibility: Immaterial Labor in Open Systems', in Joasia Krysa, op. cit.

Olga Goriunova <og@dxlab.org> is a new media curator and scholar, co-organiser of the Readme software art festivals <http://readme.runme.org>, and lecturer in new media at Moscow City University. She is completing her PhD on 'art platforms' at the Media Lab, University of Art and Design, Helsinki

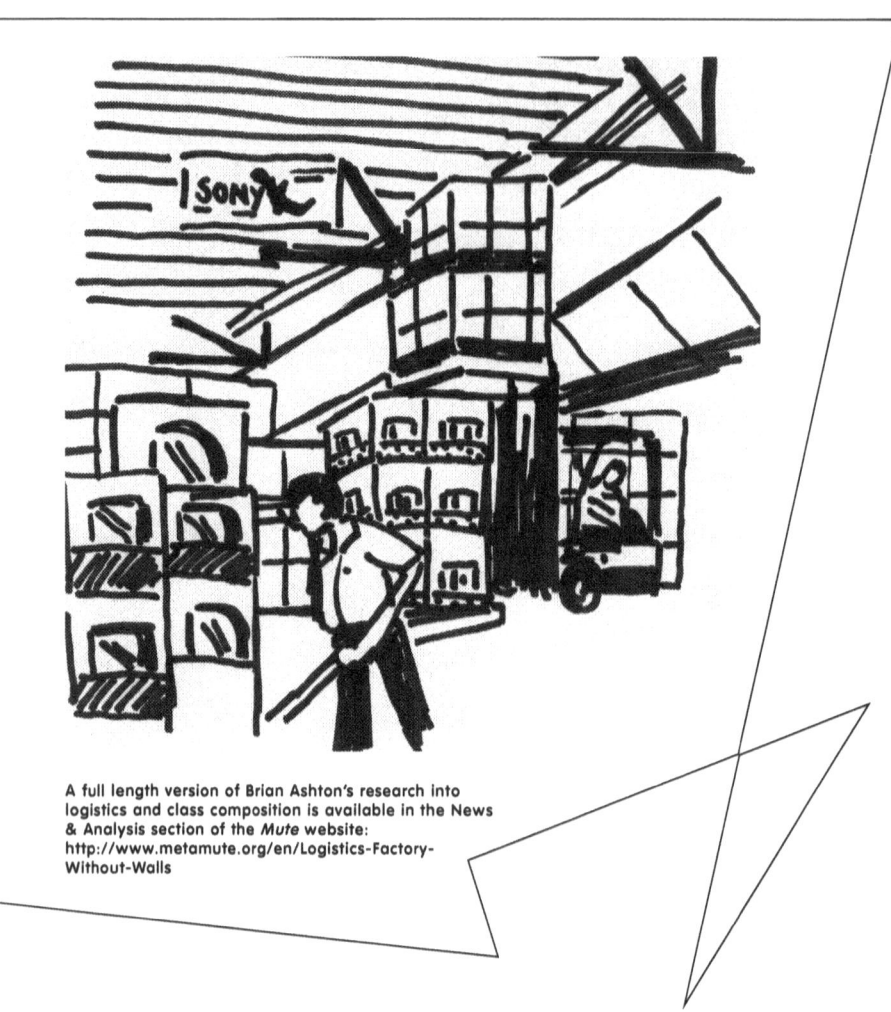

A full length version of Brian Ashton's research into
logistics and class composition is available in the News
& Analysis section of the *Mute* website:
http://www.metamute.org/en/Logistics-Factory-
Without-Walls

THE FACTORY
WITHOUT WALLS
by Brian Ashton

Images: all drawings
by Esiri Erheriene-Essi

Wireless and social networking technologies depend on and help shape the global logistics industry. This worldwide supply chain ensures just-in-time production responds to consumer demand, whether it be books from Amazon or exhaust pipes for Jaguars.

If, contra to theorists of 'immaterial labour', the mass worker is not dead but reconfigured, will networked production and distribution see the rise of networked labour struggles?

Drawing on personal experience and ongoing research, Brian Ashton gives a brief introduction to the complexities of the logistics industry

Information Technology has enabled capital to coordinate the production of commodities like never before. It is a seeming contradiction: production is spread across the globe, parts are made here and there and moved thousands of kilometres to be assembled, but this process produces more commodities than ever before. Capital has renewed itself yet again, and in the process it has thrown the left into crisis. While the talk among the intellectuals is of immaterial labour and precarity, capital is busy ironing out the kinks in its new system of production. At the same time, though, it is creating a communication system that enables workers to interact with each other across national borders and continents. Just about every worker is now an IT worker, and it is the potential that lies in this fact that poses the greatest threat to capital. It is not about immaterial or material labour. The intellectuals have got to stop creating hierarchies of labour, the mass worker and the social worker, the immaterial worker and the precariat. They would be better employed getting a proper understanding of how the supply chain – some capitalists call it the virtual enterprise – now works. Know thine enemy, as Sun Tzu said in *The Art of War*.

A team of researchers from the Cardiff Business School studied the chain of actions required to make a can of cola. The whole process, starting at the Bauxite mine in Australia and ending with the can in somebody's refrigerator took no less

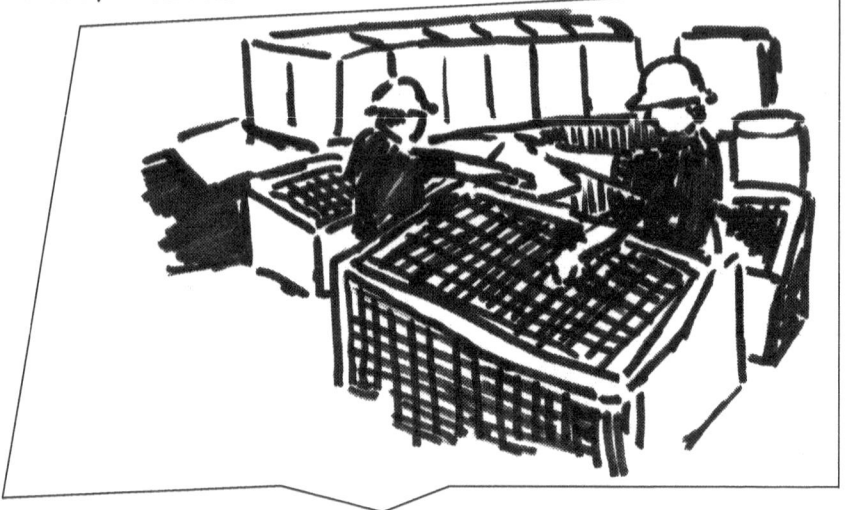

than 319 days. Of that time only three hours were spent on manufacturing, the rest was spent on transport and storage. An advertisement for the shipping company P&O Nedlloyd claims that the journey of one single container can involve literally a hundred people. These range from the guy who loaded the container to the IT people, from the logistics planners to the dockers, through the haulage drivers to the warehouse workers, from the customs officer to the captain of the ship. This highlights time and labour. The control of these two factors is the major concern for those charged with the management of supply chains.

As the Cardiff Business School study highlights, logistics is a major factor in the supply chain. According to the Council of Logistics Management, logistics is:

> the process of planning, implementing and controlling the efficient effective flow and storage of raw materials, process inventory, finished goods, extraction/production to the point of consumption.

In the last twenty years there has been a revolution in the world of logistics, a revolution that seems to have escaped the attention of the autonomous left. The cause of this upheaval was the application of technology to the globalisation of commodity production. Or as Marx put it:

A radical change in the mode of production in
one sphere of industry involves a similar change
in other spheres. This happens at first in such
branches of industry as are connected together
by being separate phases of a process, and yet are
isolated by the social division of labour, in such a
way that each of them produces an independent
commodity … But more especially, the
revolution in the modes of production of
industry and agriculture made necessary a
revolution in the general conditions of the social
process of production, i.e., in the means of
communication and transport … The means of
communication and transport were so utterly
inadequate to the productive requirements of the
manufacturing period, with its extended division
of social labour, its concentration of the
instruments of labour, and of the workmen and
its colonial markets, that they became in fact
revolutionised … And in the period of 'modern
industry' the means of communication and
transport handed down from the manufacturing
period became impediments.
Capital, vol.1, pages 262-26.

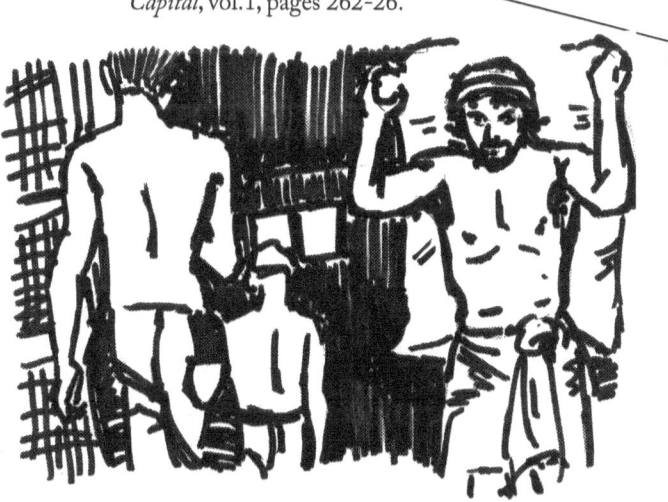

Just about every worker is now an IT worker

Autonomist marxism sees the struggle of the working class as the driver of capitalist development. In the '70s capital started to attack the concentrations of working class power that some have called the mass worker. It attacked on three fronts. It started to break up the rigidities imposed on production by working class militancy using technology to de-skill the workers and reconfigure the factory layout. It started to relocate some productive capacity to smaller sites, sub-contracting the work to other companies. And it used the state to impose crisis upon the working class. It was largely successful in its project and as the '80s developed, defeat followed defeat for the working class. A political composition forged in battle was dismantled and discarded. It seems to this old car industry worker that it wasn't only capital that discarded us but that quite a number of communist intellectuals turned their backs on us, too. The consequence is that now we have a generation of anti-capitalists who don't know how to engage with the working class. Despite being surrounded by the class they seem more interested in what goes on in the Mexican jungle, or prefer to go to Genoa and Seattle and give the state

machine an opportunity to practice crowd control.

In the '60s and '70s there was constant interaction between working class militants and the left emerging from the universities. This wasn't always positive, but, where there was a synergy, theory and practice had some connection. We learned from each other and good work was produced. Here in Britain work published by Solidarity and Big Flame is evidence of that. In Italy Potere Operaio and Lotta Continua helped to develop an understanding of the strengths and weaknesses of capital's composition. Today we may talk about a globalised production system but how many of us can describe how it works? How does the can of cola get from A to Z? In the '70s we knew how the factory and the transport systems worked and in that knowledge lay our ability to combat capital. Today, it is certainly difficult to grasp exactly how things are made, but it is imperative that we gain deep knowledge of the processes of production and logistics, the supply chains of capital or, to put it another way, the factories without walls. Some capitalists see the supply chain as a virtual factory and want workers to relate to the supply chain rather than perceiving themselves as employees of the separate organisations that make the chain up.

Working class composition comes from struggle, but first capitalists have to bring the workers together and impose the discipline of production upon them.

In the present period we can only understand how that discipline is imposed if we take a global approach. The technical composition of capital is spread across the world, as are the workers in the commodity's supply chain. Discipline under such a system is imposed through the application of *kaizen* (continuous improvement) and just-in-time stock delivery combined with the application of information technologies that police the workers' productivity.

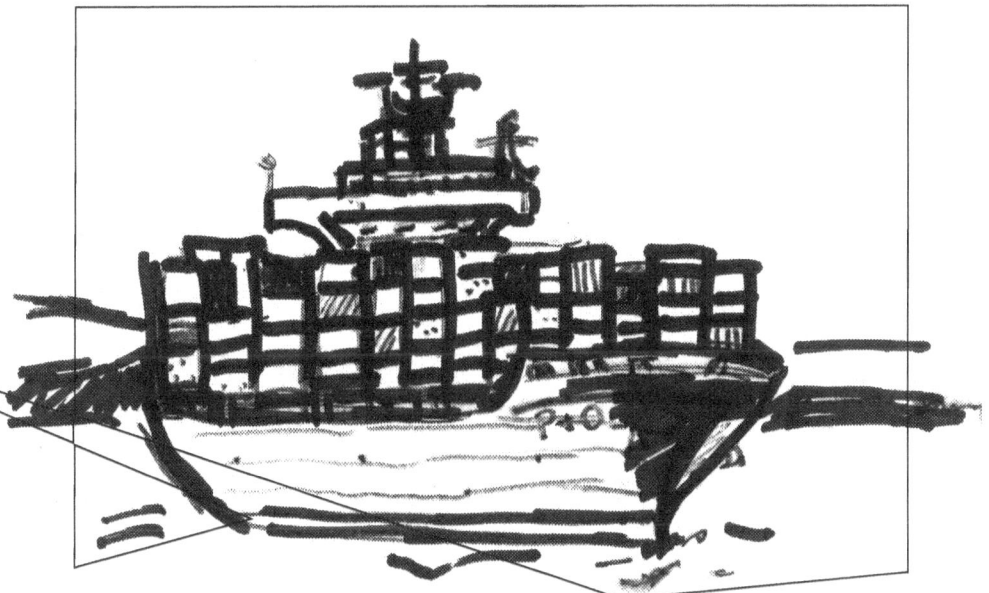

This is reinforced by the change in how commodities are moved through the system. Capital has moved from a push to a pull economy, in other words, it is making things that are being demanded rather than making them to forecast demand. The motto of the pull economy could be, 'If it isn't sold, don't make another one.' The pull economy gives the big supermarket chains enormous power because they control the information that pulls a commodity through the supply chain. When you buy a tin of beans in Asda the information is sent out to all those along the chain in order for another tin of

information technologies police workers' productivity

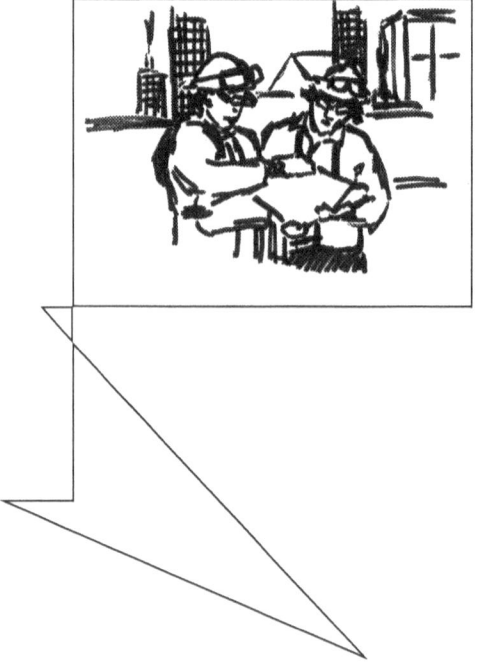

beans to be produced. Of course, millions of such pieces of information are flying through cyberspace every moment of the day. One of the results of the pull economy is an increase in precarious work: if demand is down then lay off workers. Companies have computer programs that calculate the number of workers needed to satisfy a given demand, drawing in extra workers from a pool of casual labour, often supplied by employment agencies. And increasingly they outsource non-core activities to service companies; this is one of the reasons for the mushrooming of the logistics industry in these last years. The automotive industry is moving to a pull economy model and this is one of the main reasons autoworkers in the States are being battered at the moment.

If you spread your supply chains across the globe and reduce your stock levels to just-in-time then you increase the importance of the logistical exercise in the completion of the cycle of accumulation. At the same time you increase the possibility of effective working class struggle: when the truckers on the west coast of the USA struck a year or so back they paralysed the supply chains of Wal-Mart and other chain store giants, sending waves of panic through many a boardroom. The importance of logistics cannot be overestimated; try imagining the supply chain of any product without the logistical input. The globalisation of production has left many workers believing they can do nothing about it when companies move production to China or India, they stand hypnotised by the lights on the capitalist juggernaut as it runs them over, but this *apparent* strength of multinational capital is *in fact* its weakness.

Historically, logistics workers have been carriers of radical thought and transporters of the news of working class struggles. They have, of course, been involved in many a battle themselves. In the last twenty years many of those battles have been defensive, fighting to save jobs and maintain working conditions. The withdrawal of the state from the direct management of the logistics industry was the catalyst for a global attack that continues to this day. As the state withdrew, private capital stepped into the breech and attacked workforces throughout the industry. At the same time these companies have been engaged in a frenzy of mergers and acquisitions that have resulted in the emergence of truly global organisations employing many thousands of workers.

Some idea of the size of these companies can be gleaned from two examples, United Parcel Services (UPS) and Deutsche Post (DP). UPS is a 33.5 billion dollar company that operates in 200 countries and employs more than 340,000 workers. It provides transportation and freight logistics/distribution, international trade, financial services, financial mail facilities and consultancy services. It has grown by benefiting from the outsourcing processes that are common in industry and by acquiring other companies. It plays for big stakes: it bought the Fritz freight company for 450 million dollars. DP is partly owned by the German government, who hold 41.6 percent of the shares. These will be sold to institutional investors over the next few years. DP runs the German postal service, owns DHL, and last year it bought the British registered company Exel. Exel was an acquisitive company itself before being bought out; it had previously bought Tibbett&Britten, the seventh biggest logistics company in the world. This resulted in a company employing more than 103,000 people. I don't know how many people work for DP, but it must be in the hundreds of thousands.

The Jaguar auto plant in Halewood on Merseyside can perhaps give us an idea of how a supply chain works and how logistics fits into the chain. Halewood was where Ford built the Escort, and where this proletarian worked for seven long years. It was regarded as the basket case of the Ford organisation and the threat of closure was always hanging over it. Ford bought Jaguar and decided to manufacture Jags at Halewood, at the same time it decided to radically alter working practices in the plant. It brought in an American company called Senn-Delaney to alter the mindset of the workforce, and it appears to have been successful because Halewood is now regarded as the best car plant in Europe. If such a company had been brought in during the '70s their work would have been challenged by counter-information from the left.

When I worked in Halewood in the '70s there were 14,000 of us employed on the site. Today Jaguar employs some 2,800 people, but this figure is deceptive because a sizable chunk of the work has been hived off to suppliers who in turn pass some of the work on to smaller suppliers. In a supply chain firms are categorised thus: Original Equipment Manufacturer (OEM), i.e. Jaguar; First Tier Supplier, i.e. Bosch; the smaller suppliers are called second tier, third tier, etc. Linking all these together are the logistics companies. At Halewood UCI Logistics, a subsidiary of the Japanese company Nippon Yusen Kaisha (NYK) runs the logistical set up. As lead logistics supplier, UCI is responsible for inbound logistics to Halewood as well as the internal logistics at the plant itself. In the Ford days internal logistics would have been carried out by Ford workers. The inbound logistics service involves a supply chain operation and the collection of parts and sub-assemblies from suppliers around Europe partly using their own fleet and partly UCI Logistics-appointed partners. The internal logistics service involves offloading parts, movement of components to storage areas and making them available to the production lines without incurring line-side storage. It is also UCI's task to ensure that line-side stock never exceeds the two-hour volume Jaguar has stipulated. It is UCI workers who drive the fork lift trucks that transfer material within the Halewood plant.

Let's look at the logistics of a particular product going into Halewood, the wheel and tyre assemblies. UCI moves 500,000 assemblies a year into Halewood. The contract includes both external logistics for the supply of alloy wheels from Italy to Pirelli's facility in the UK and the delivery of completed assemblies to Halewood, three times a day, together with the internal logistics at the Jaguar site. UCI chooses from twelve different types of assemblies on receiving automated instructions from Jaguar and delivers the product to the point of fit. The mass worker hasn't been destroyed s/he has just been reconfigured.

Capital gets its power from the extraction of surplus value and the supply chain is the factory without walls where this process takes place. In the past socialists organised and agitated around the centres of commodity production – one thinks of the work done around Fiat's Mirafiori factory in Turin and Big Flame's efforts at Dagenham and Halewood – but is that sort of work going on today? If such agitation is to take place it will have to be on a global scale, but the technology exists to do it. By going global with its supply chains, capital is creating the opportunity for global working class struggle. In order for such struggles to succeed we need to know how the

the journey of one single container can involve literally a hundred people

present composition of capital works. The craft worker and the mass worker knew how the system produced commodities in their day; we need to develop such knowledge today.

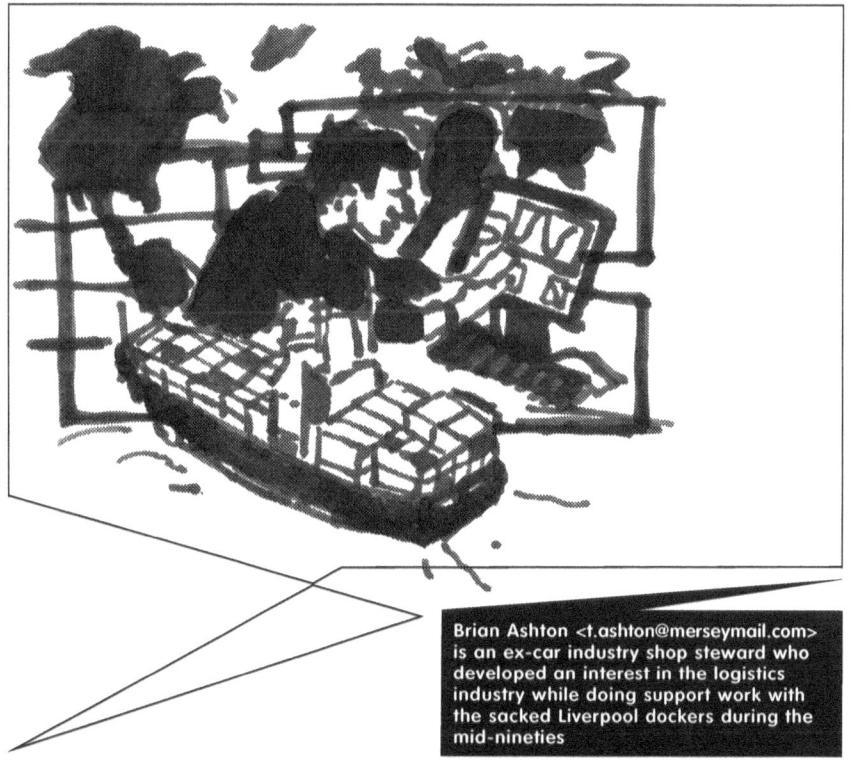

Brian Ashton <t.ashton@merseymail.com> is an ex-car industry shop steward who developed an interest in the logistics industry while doing support work with the sacked Liverpool dockers during the mid-nineties

Free improvisation guitarist and theorist Derek Bailey could be described as the Samuel Beckett of post-war music. Bailey moved nohow-onward by means of a continually repeated negation of the familiar, eschewing the idiomatic for the (almost) uncommodifiably new. Ben Watson's biography of Bailey, published earlier this year, celebrates the life and unfinishable works of an avant garde anti-artist. But, asks Paul Helliwell, do Bailey and Watson throw too much musical baby out with the tonal bathwater? And where does the increasingly venerable practice of free improvisation stand in relation to modernism's dialectic of the new today?

FIRST CUT IS THE DEEPEST
by Paul Helliwell

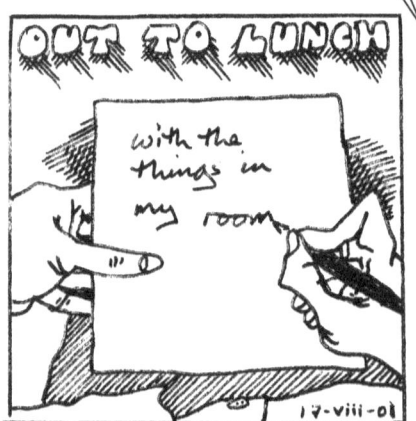

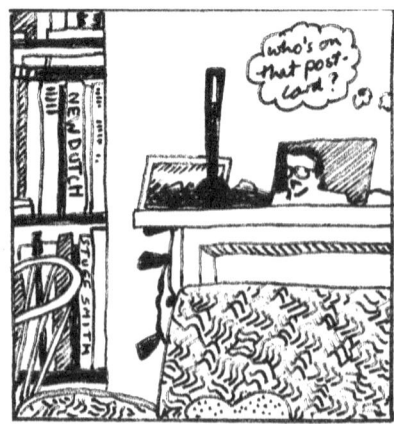

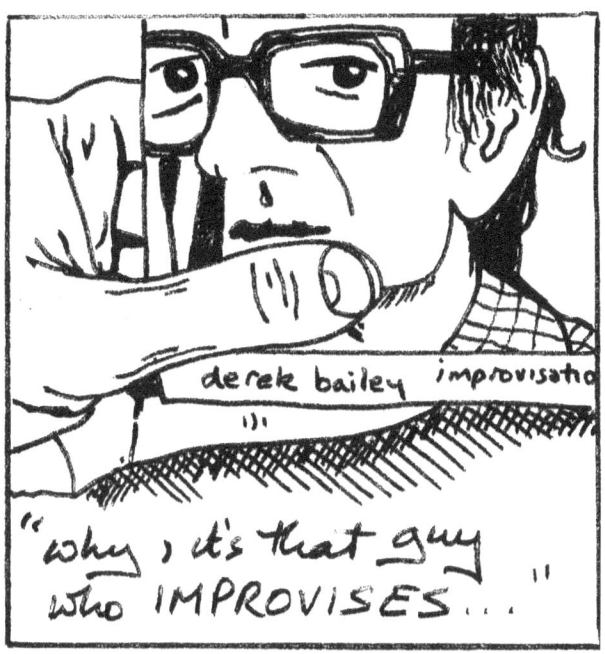

derek bailey improvisatio

"why, it's that guy who IMPROVISES..."

Form deforms
– Witold Gombrowicz

We have to give the truth to this man, he's a serious journalist and biographer
– Derek Bailey on Ben Watson

The best argument Derek Bailey knew against Improvisation, based on his experiences playing guitar for wrestling matches, was a huge wrestler upset with the way he'd just played 'Enter the Gladiators'. Like this example, and like free improvisation itself, by far the best bits of Ben Watson's *Derek Bailey and the Story of Free Improvisation*, are conversations. These conversations Watson recorded himself with many of the key players in the scene; the book is Watson's conversation with these recordings. There is a happy danger the book could come to resemble the ideal improv situation where even the players are unsure who played what – where the conversation 'comes alive'.

Improvisers, both musical and theatrical, make of the present moment an inverse black hole, a magician's top hat, out of which, seemingly from nothing and faster than thought, can

Images: Ben Watson, *Bailey - a Cartoon.* Thanks to Ben for letting us reproduce the images here.

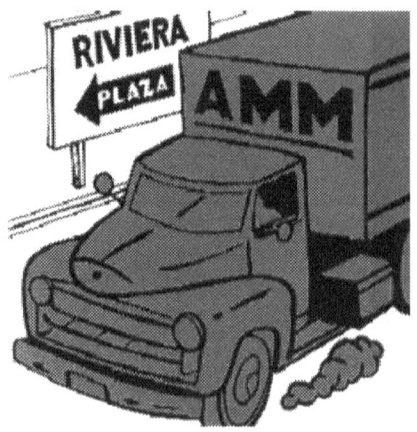

Watson writes, he tells us, imagining free improvisers looking over his shoulder

be pulled new and marvellous things. Facing each other, the musicians pull things from their top hats, like an expanded game of scissors, paper, stone. We laugh and gasp in recognition as the recently new things are reincorporated into new contexts. Yet, to make these moments possible, a strict co-operation must be maintained. There is no time for reflection and censorship, the content must be left to look after itself. Later, the practice of this creation is generalised into an ideology that the content, the 'finished product', be a matter of indifference.

For listeners, music is a flash art – one that happens in the present moment as we hear it and understand its structure – and Improvisers wish its creation to be likewise. Other than Derek Bailey, few have written on musical improvisation as a practice. His book, *Improvisation: Its Nature and Practice in Music*, reveals how much improvisation goes on within forms of music we already know, ones that obey genre rules of musical

signification (idiomatic music – flamenco, jazz, church organ playing) and thus render non-idiomatic or free improvisation familiar. Bailey argues that for playing 'free' to be successful, the process of improvisation must exclude these idiomatic elements, genre conventions. Arising from practice, this is a modernist argument on music's need to pursue its own formal autonomy.

One difficulty for Ben Watson's book lies in the limitations of free improvisation and of conversation. Neither copes well with the introduction of predetermined material. Watson says, 'Bailey's position is ultimately compatible with my own Musical Marxism but I don't expect him to say so' and gives his reasons:

> Theory and abstraction are immediately suspicious to Bailey, they freeze the moment, generalise the instant, abuse the actuality, bully the musician.

Watson even reflects this himself: 'generalities rarely provide answers (rather they stifle examination of particulars by reference to ideology).'

Image: *AMMMusic* by AMM, album cover, 1966

Bailey wants to leave the moment gritty and unassimilable – for this grit makes the pearl – What does Watson want?

These mirrored caveats are in fact a sales pitch, but also, to mix metaphors, a punch Watson pulls. Out of respect for the structure of conversation/ free improv itself, Watson doesn't bring theory – specifically that of Theodor Adorno – to the table like he promises in the text and in the bibliography. Perhaps I am taxing him with what was never his intention, or perhaps there were forces beyond his control. Watson writes as if torn between the improvising community, his own (somewhat equivocal) commitment to Adorno and his duties as a biographer. He writes, he tells us, imagining free improvisers looking over his shoulder.

As the translator of Adorno's *Aesthetic Theory* explains:

> Every translation must fit one world inside another, but not every work to be translated has been shaped by emphatic opposition to the world into which it must be fitted.

This is the orientation of the free improvisers (to the act of improvising itself not the recording) and of Adorno (to the work and not to the reader), and both can be seen as a resistance to commodity status. This task is Watson's also, to fit the free improvisational moment into a biography, into record appreciation, and to re-orient it towards his readers – in particular the free-improvising community, whose story he tells.

Gavin Bryars is an interesting voice within this book. This is not, as Watson argues, despite his defection from Free Improvisation to Composition but because of it. Watson's question, 'It's as if you and Derek worked out your musical philosophies by contradicting each other', briefly holds out the possibility of a Schoenberg/ Stravinsky face off in the manner of Adorno's *Philosophy of Modern Music*. But it is not to be, Watson has used this tactic before and anyway, for Watson's assumed audience of pro-Bailey free improvisers, Bryars is persona non grata. Instead, Watson takes repeated stabs at Bryars for accepting commissions as if Adorno had not noted that subsidy and patronage are a feature of everything labelled

Music says 'we', even when it is irredeemably difficult and unpopular

esoteric under commodity culture, as if 'earning it's own living' proved anything aesthetically, as if improv had never received Arts Council grants. Tellingly, Bryars' response to this is to continue to insist on the contradictions between Improvisation and Composition, refusing to be summed up as the anti-Bailey and thus blocked (very Bailey). He plays scissors to Watson's paper.

Watson is loyal to Bailey, but once we've moved on from Bailey's early years, from the jobbing danceband musician, from the glory days of the Joseph Holbrooke Trio (founded by Bailey with bassist Bryars and drummer Tony Oxley), the story is over. Even Bailey is ambivalent about the improv 'scene' and its continued survival. Watson consistently fails to interrogate practices within this story of free improvisation that contradict Bailey's vision. Improv's bruising encounters with dada/fluxus/performance art that disrupt the (for Bailey) necessary co-operation between players, the practice of improvising to recordings of other improvisers, the 'contribution' of 'bargers-in', and lastly the status of recordings

themselves are all passed over. As a paid 'reviewer of records' and yet despiser of commodities, this last one at least should interest Watson. But these are merely listed: gigs you should've been at; CDs you should own (and simultaneously should not, or maybe could on auratic vinyl); and, as if performances were not commodities, yearly shareholders reports from Company Week, the annual London improv event Bailey helped run.

The most organised contradiction is mentioned obliquely, namely the 31st March 1984 Association of Improvised Music (AIM) Forum, Improvisation: History, Directions and Practice. At this event, practising improvisers Eddie Prévost and Andy Hamilton held that habits and conventions attending the performance become idiom (just as Adorno argues that form is sedimented content). More seriously, for Prévost, Bailey's *Improvisation: It's Nature and Practice in Music* had erroneously tried to make non-idiomatic improvisation an 'agreed objective'. This is the ideological fault line of the scene, and Watson knows it, having been 'the subject of a furious public dressing down' by Evan Parker (uninterviewed – the commissar vanishes) for criticising the use of tonal material in an improvisation. With a charming rhetorical flourish, Watson affects to be so disgusted by these refusals to accept free improvisation's modernist agenda (this Stravinskyite 'self-conscious revocation of musical knowledge' as Adorno might say) that he is unable to review the Company Week featuring

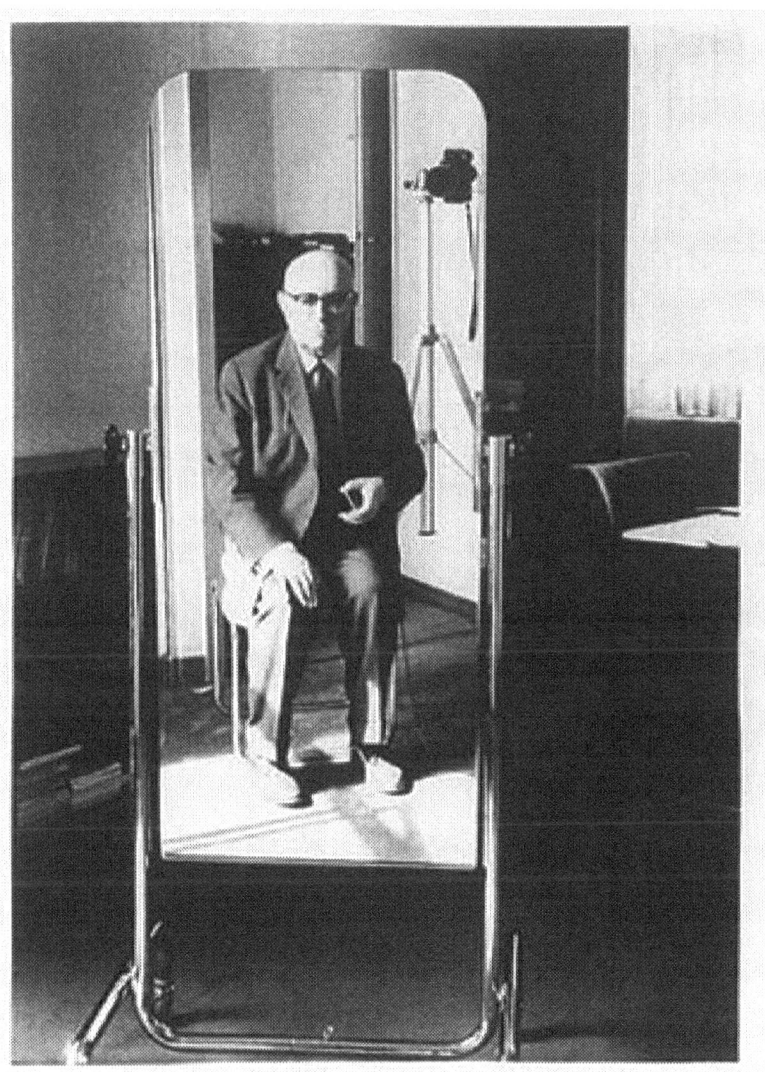

these key AIM musicians – many of whom have now gone on to become the mainstream of free improvisation.

To fit the worlds of free improvisation and book publishing inside each other Watson has relied on a readymade structure of biography, and in particular Frank Kofsky's *Black Nationalism and the Revolution in Music*, but in its re-issued and zombiefied form:

Image: Theodor W.
Adorno, *Self-portrait*,
photo by Stefan Moses,
1963

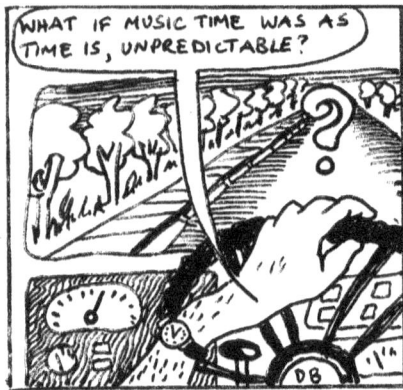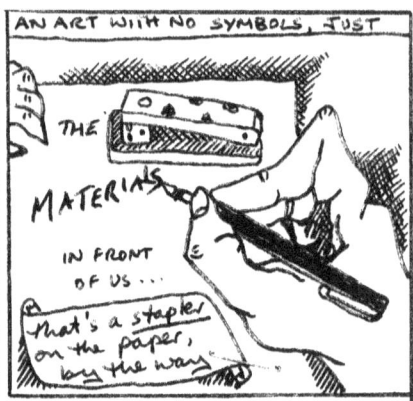

John Coltrane and the Jazz Revolution of the 1960s. As with improvisation, the first cut is the deepest. Just compare these titles and Watson's title, they're a fair summary of what lies within and the historical tendency to atomisation. In the later book, the chapter on the economic injustices of the jazz industry has been hived off into a separate (and thinner) book *Black Music, White Business*, and replaced by the (personality) cult of John Coltrane. As Kofsky, Leroi Jones (Amiri Baraka), and Francis Newton (E.J. Hobsbawm) noted, other than Bill Evans (and perhaps Bix Beiderbecke), innovation in Jazz is down to black people, but the business and critical apparatus of it remained in the hands of whites. Kofsky uses Marx and Engels' dictum that, under capitalism, ideologically all things appear 'upside down as in a camera obscura' to explain the inversion of the role of Black musicians within Jazz – both critically and economically. Indeed Pathfinder Press have taken this to heart and bound my copy of *Black Nationalism* upside down within its cover.

Let us take this insight further and apply it to free improvisation – let us invert that moment.

The moment of free improvisation is precisely and only free because the rest of time and volition is in chains. The autonomy of free improv is created by the exclusion of idiomatic music, conventional moments of musical signification, theory, levels of language other than musical ones. A lot of baby has been thrown out with the bathwater to make these moments possible – and if Adorno is correct, like the 1910 revolutionary art movements, free improvisers are experiencing not new freedoms but more things 'constantly pulled into the vortex of the newly taboo'. In this light, the Association of Improvised Music's objections to Bailey's exclusion of the idiomatic become an understandable (if futile), defence of the scene.

Yet, according to Christophe Mencke, in his *The Sovereignty of Art*,

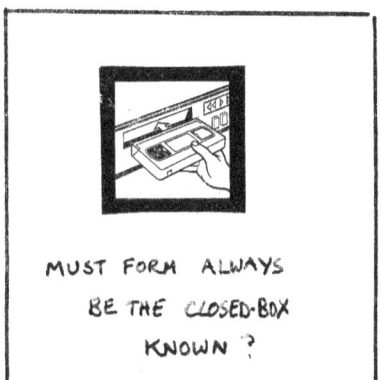

MUST FORM ALWAYS
BE THE CLOSED-BOX
KNOWN ?

Once upon a time, music was held to be autonomous, its own discourse within the field of reason governed by its own laws and not determined by some other realm, economics for instance. However, these laws gradually ruled more and more things taboo until what was easy and natural had to be abandoned and replaced with what was difficult and unpleasant. This trajectory can be found in Adorno's *Philosophy of Modern Music*, Witold Gombrowicz's *Diaries* and Leroi Jones' *Blues People*. It cost classical music in Europe not just it's audience but also its social effect, this music ceased to be at the heart of the culture, just as BeBop did.

However, it is also claimed that music and art are sovereign, that they can exceed the bounds that reason sets them, they can be transcendent, and make the infinite present. Music says 'we', even when it is irredeemably difficult and unpopular, due to its cultic origin, as does art. This is the revolutionary potential of art and music, not as propaganda or recruiting sergeant but as offering a vision of a re-centred totality. Yet this has become a difficult claim to make.

these discourses smuggle within them Adorno's antinomy of aesthetic semblance: not only does 'form deform', suicide by music's own laws of development, by its autonomy – but also music has a real social effect deriving from its truth value – it is sovereign.

There is a duality to the modern view of aesthetic experience (and thus to modern views on music). On the one hand it is one discourse among many, adhering to its own internal logic, possessing no negating or affirming powers over non-aesthetic experience (and vice versa) – autonomy; on the other, it exceeds the bounds of its discourse, it is granted not just a relative validity within its own discourse but an absolute one – it becomes 'the vehicle for an experientially enacted critique of reason' – sovereignty. On the face of it both cannot hold simultaneously, yet Adorno links these by the Kantian concept of antinomy, arguing that for a full understanding both must be present and neither must be sacrificed to the other.

The problem for people engaged in making radical claims for music is that autonomy and sovereignty are now seen as opposites that annihilate rather than as an antinomy, and that the critical terms themselves have fallen into disuse and are viewed only as nostalgia. The intellectual position of the arts (and in particular music) has fallen; nowadays we are merely on our knees before them as irrationality, without any understanding of how we got there.

What can be done when almost everything has been pulled into the void? Derek Bailey was a fan of Sam Beckett, as was Adorno who wished to dedicate *Aesthetic Theory* to him. Adorno's discussion of Beckett and of the new sees him as the key to (then – 1969) contemporary anti-art in 'culling aesthetic meaning from the radical negation of aesthetic meaning', making an art 'trying to pull itself free from its own concept as from a shackle.' Content becomes opaque, becomes a critique of the omnipotence of reason, interpretation must be refused. This fits in all too well with Bailey's resistant reticence on free improvisation (stone to scissors), but also leads to a monolithic inability to move beyond it.

If music is no longer its own realm or 'secret regent' of this one, one consequence is that, as Jacques Attali predicted in *Noise*, it must be made to do work, or pressed into service: as Ben Watson says, 'Free music is the song of the New International'.

There is in Adorno's writings a tendency to make aesthetic negativity into social critique (and this is why we like him, despite his writing like 'a coroner performing an autopsy'). When reading Watson's 'Music, Violence, Truth', an account of the debates surrounding radical music post 9/11, we see how heteronymously overburdened aesthetic negativity has become. For Watson 'The crucial point is that art is an attempt to tell the truth about the world, not simply to provide baubles for those in the comfort zone of privilege.' Surely art must be capable of doing other things as well. Indeed this pamphlet gives us a vision of this radical art in the fleshy golem that Ben Watson rhetorically constructs out of just the right proportions of Coltrane, Hendrix, Tony Oxley and Cecil Taylor – a piece of paper on the truth value of art in its mouth (Emeth). Yet to construct this Frankenstein requires violence, witness, 'Varese brought the noise of sirens and bombs into music in the 1920s, a response to the terrors of World War 1.' This distorts Varese's real and formal motivation – the need for new musical instruments.

Watson ostentatiously celebrates the contradictory, unfinished nature of his text, pleading the pressure of biography but knowing that he smuggles his musical marxism within it. His method is more Benjamin than Adorno, he needs this conversation between his marxism and his music to come alive. However, in the absence of dialectic to do some housekeeping, the real contradictions get lost in the clutter of allegedly auratic stockpiled free improv commodities.

The very productivity of improvisation is a problem. The early theatrical improvisers, in particular Keith Johnstone, emphasised it's pedagogic value in awakening children's imaginations that had been blunted by education. Yet when they set up performing ensembles they chose ambivalent names such as Theatre Machine. Improvisation leads to an embarrassment of riches, and both derive from its automatism. Critically, for the logic of capitalism, what it generates are new things. If capitalism has already appropriated the irrationality of music, it has also appropriated this productivity: *Kid A*, *Big Brother*, *Baddiel and Skinner Unplanned* and indeed jazz itself. Maybe Adorno is just clearer about this than we permit ourselves to be.

Watson is right, in his introduction and text, to attempt to forestall the 'gruesomely predictable' objections repeated here, and yet these cracks reach the surface because they arise from contradictions between free improvisation itself and the world as a whole. If Watson does not cast a string of pearls out of this grit with a single blow of his magic hammer it is because the material doesn't play that way. Difficulty is so valuable it must sometimes be smuggled.

How does modern aesthetic reflection deal with this situation? Dan Fox's excellent appreciation of Derek Bailey in *frieze* magazine (March 2006) notes the 'romantic excitement' generated about free improvisation's 'uncommodifiability', but he prefers to view it as functioning as a 'kind of relational aesthetics for music'. Freed from notions of the antinomy of autonomy and sovereignty, Bourriaud's relational aesthetics itself functions by a panglossian inversion of Gombrowicz's notion of interpersonal form – 'for Gombrowicz, our "form" is merely a relational property, linking us with those who reify us by the way they see us, to borrow a Sartrian terminology...' Yet, for Gombrowicz this 'form deforms', the

form imposed on us by others has to be struggled against. His *Diaries* and his appreciation of Sandaeur, the critic who defended his reputation in Poland, testify to this at length. For Bourriaud the interpersonal form is the substrate of art. Like AIM's admission of tonal material and idiomatic improvisation, this is a strategy for continuing the game, but with no autonomy to move it forward, there's no development. 'The new is no longer a criterion...' My editor asks me how different is this from Beckett's 'nothing new'? I don't know, yet. The one may simply be the critical apparatus for the other.

The theatrical improvisers teach us that by reincorporation, by 'tying up loose ends', the story is brought to a close. One ending suggests itself: 'Derek Bailey is dead and the story of free improvisation is over', but this does not do justice to the energies emerging from the improvisational moment. Instead I return to our huge upset wrestler. He removes his top hat (didn't I mention that?), and pulls from it... a marvellous thing... something gritty... it is a copy of *Derek Bailey and the Story of Free Improvisation* by Ben Watson.

Info:
Ben Watson, *Derek Bailey and the Story of Free Improvisation*, Verso, 2004

Paul Helliwell <phelliwell2000@yahoo.co.uk> would like to direct people to the MySpace site of his 'brother ass' horsemouth, www.myspace.com/horsemouthfolk

EXTREME MAKEOVER
by Merijn Oudenampsen

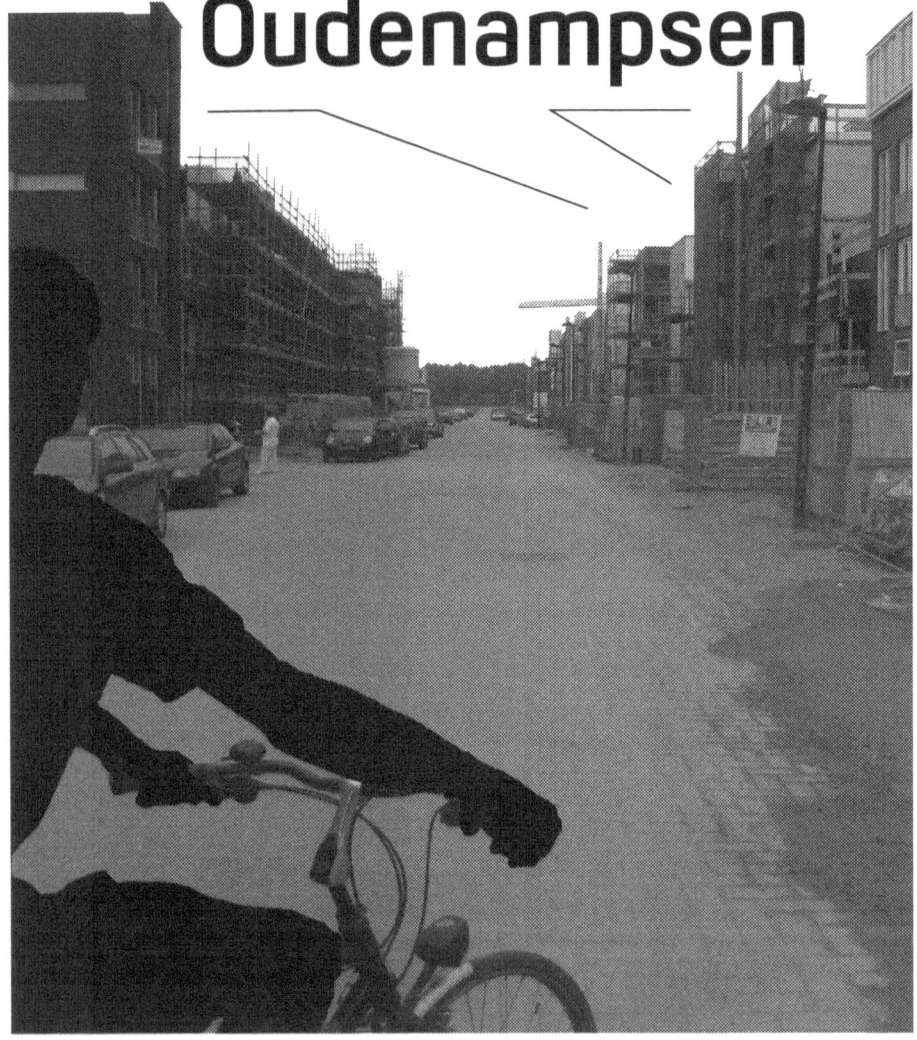

Images of the I amsterdam branding campaign by
Merijn Oudenampsen (M.O.) and of IJburg, a new,
model Amsterdam community by Pauline van
Mourik Broekman (P.v.M.B)

Amsterdam is undergoing a historic process of regeneration. Much of the city's reserve of social housing is being transformed into luxury accommodation for the growing numbers of 'creative economy' employees. Meanwhile, waiting lists for the remaining social housing are flooded by former occupants forced out of their homes and neighbourhoods by renovation programmes. Merijn Oudenampsen describes a process of urban 'rebirth' through place branding and social cleansing

This is a new version of a text originally published in the Dutch language *Flexmens* Magazine

Do not start with the good old things; start with the bad new ones
– Bertolt Brecht

According to a recent report by the Amsterdam city council, in coming years more houses are going to be demolished than ever before in the turbulent history of this town. It is the so-called 'restructuring neighbourhoods', poor areas such as Westelijke Tuinsteden, Noord en de Bijlmermeer, where most of the houses will have a close encounter with the wrecking ball. The pre-war neighbourhoods, such as the Staatsliedenbuurt, the Oosterparkbuurt, the Indische Buurt or the Kinkerbuurt are the subject of thorough renovations.[1] Overall, tens of thousands of social housing apartments will disappear to make way for the sand blasted facades that distinguish the homes of the new middle class.

This development isn't restricted to Amsterdam. Minister Dekker's national housing policy underlines the need to 'differentiate' and to 'socially mix', or, in other words, move higher earners into the poor neighbourhoods where social housing predominates. Although sociological research has yet been unable to prove any of its alleged social mobility-boosting effects, social mixing is – according to Dekker's urban planners

– a potent means to deal with the social problems of 'backward' neighbourhoods. The perverse logic of the urban renewal plans is that the less well-off inhabitants of the 'backward' neighbourhoods, who are supposed to be the beneficiaries of the policy, are also its main victims. Large proportions of neighbourhood residents are being forced to leave when their houses are renovated as luxury apartments. The Turkish grocery stores and their patrons are being forced to make way for the beauty salons, art galleries and boutiques servicing a very different demographic.

Underneath the inflated rhetoric of social mixing, where terms such as social integration, upward mobility and cultural diversity predominate, there is another agenda. It's an agenda filled with the sober calculation of economic interests. Since its partial privatisation in 1994, social housing corporations are themselves solely responsible for balancing their budgets, and are allowed to compensate for the loss of state subsidies by selling off social housing stock. In the current urban renewal process they do so with enthusiasm.[2]

However, to be able to sell or rent the houses for the appropriate price, the area has to be made attractive for new arrivals. Publicity campaigns are set up, PR agencies too, cultural festivals and poetry readings take place, artists are offered temporary residence; everything is done to change the image of the area from that of a loose cohabitation of immigrants, unemployed, elderly, and other economic losers to the image of a dynamic and cultural hot spot, pervaded by the buzz of renewal. This is the place to be.

The I amsterdam Model

The urban renewal plans are part and parcel of a bigger metamorphosis of the city, preparing it for the 'creative era'. In an age in which the creative knowledge economy has allegedly become the most important economic sector, it is the creative, highly educated and talented workforce – the creative class – that decides the economic destiny of cities. Allegedly, this new class is also extremely mobile and savvy about its choice of city. Amsterdam is thus competing with other international metropoles – London, Barcelona, Berlin – to lure creatives with culturally interesting surroundings and the quality of its urban habitat. Amsterdam, not wanting to fall behind, brands itself as a 'Creative Knowledge City' and starts the marketing campaign 'I amsterdam'.[3] While art and culture never rated high on the aldermen's priority list, they have suddenly gained central importance in the marketing offensive.

The urban planners have no reason to complain. The amount of Amsterdammers earning double the mean income has risen in the short period from 1999 to 2003 from 10.8% to 18%. Amsterdam gentrifies. As a result, space is becoming more and more expensive in the city, which means that it is now more attractive to sell some of the social housing in the popular neighbourhoods. Another consequence of the city's economic success is that the city edge, previously the territory of a frivolously experimental group of artists and squatters, is being replaced with a sterile environment of high priced houses and architecturally unimaginative glass-surfaced shoebox offices. The eviction of the squatted warehouse Pakhuis Afrika for the docklands spectacle, Sail 2005, marked the completion of this transition.[4]

The influential ideologue of Amsterdam Creative City, social geographer Sako Musterd, states in his research that one of the shortcomings of Amsterdam is a lack of proper housing for the creative class. The Amsterdam business community – represented through the chamber of commerce – goes one step further, stating in their press communiqués that the less educated have to leave town to make space for creativity to move in. Politicians and bureaucrats have meanwhile reinvented themselves as true entrepreneurs. Mayor Cohen speaks about the Amsterdam brand, the city is being run as a business, and branding has grown to become the new *maakbaarheid*.[5]

This new urban management, which I have called the 'I amsterdam model', has also reached the neighbourhood level. City regions are competing for the attention of the more highly educated middle class in the attempt to secure their own economic success. Every neighbourhood organises cultural events, Westerpark has the Westergasfabriek, the Kinkerbuurt has de Hallen, Noord the former NDSM warf, the Indische Buurt the Timor-school and even in the notoriously boring suburban area of the Kolenkitbuurt in Bos en Lommer, apartments are being sold with the mention of new cultural establishments in the vicinity.

Housing Shortage

Under the I amsterdam banner a radically different form of urban management and renewal has arrived. Old architecture is being upgraded or completely demolished and, in parallel, accounts are being settled with the ideas and ideals present at the foundation of the previous architectural regime. From the red-brick-socialism of architect Berlage, Le Corbusier's dys-functionalist utopia of reinforced concrete as embodied in the flats of the Bijlmermeer and the Parisian banlieux, to the 'bouwen voor de buurt' of alderman Schaeferi, the history of urban renewal is filled with the hope of achieving the elevation of the people, of emancipation through the drawing board.[6] In the '70s a new set of ideals saw integration, upward mobility and emancipation taking place at neighbourhood level, with the assistance of an entire infrastructure of neighbourhood centres and social workers.

I amsterdam's current regime of urban rebirth has abandoned these concepts. Poverty can be moved – distributed – but not remedied. While hitherto urban renewal targeted the lower classes, the new urban renewal is directed

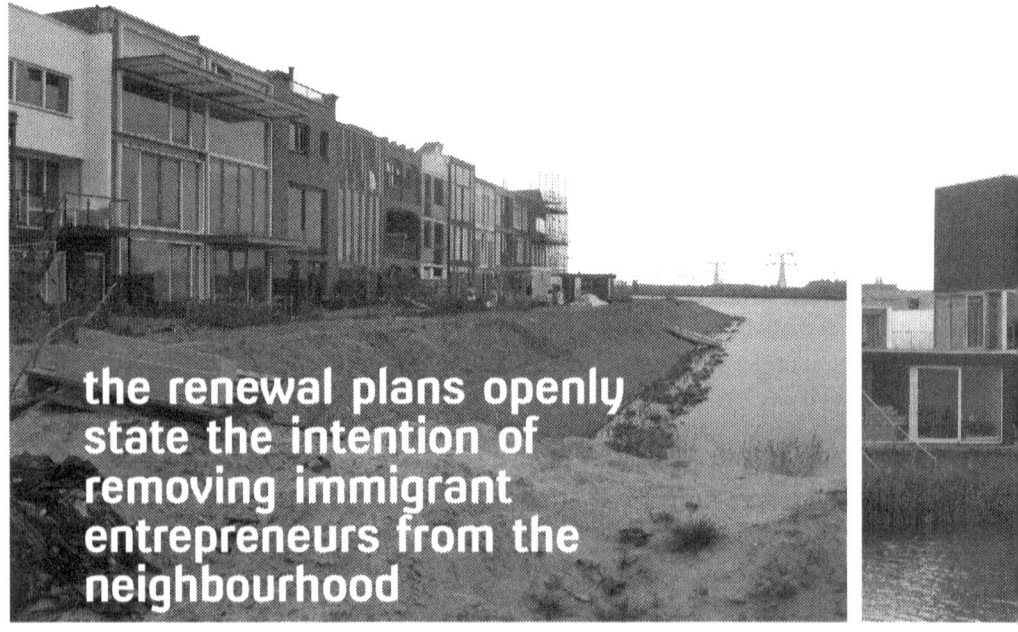

the renewal plans openly
state the intention of
removing immigrant
entrepreneurs from the
neighbourhood

Images: P.v.M.B.

towards the middle class, that is, it functions as a Trojan horse to reconquer the poor neighbourhoods and expropriate property from their inhabitants. The ex-occupants are offered financial compensation; for most, the direct personal impact is a rent increase or the obligation to relocate. Nonetheless, displacement of a whole stratum of the population is the result. What makes the Dutch gentrification process so subtle, is that the effect is indirect: due to the many displaced residents being conferred priority status for rehousing, those without it have to wait even longer for social housing. Hence, the worst effects are displaced onto others, especially younger generations and newcomers to the city. For students in Amsterdam, large temporary container housing projects have been built.

The developments in the Indische Buurt in Amsterdam are a good example. The neighbourhood is one of the areas that will be given a thorough facelift in the

coming years. About 20 percent of social housing (2,000 apartments) will disappear through demolition, conversion and renovation. Change in the composition of the neighbourhood's predominantly immigrant population is officially the most important goal, and urban renewal thus becomes a form of social and racial engineering through state-led gentrification.[7]

Planners from the local council state that the new neighbourhood policy is no longer about 'fighting problems', but 'the creation of opportunities'. It is this kind of vague language that legitimises large amounts of money earmarked for backward neighbourhoods being spent on marketing campaigns and subsidised business locations for creative entrepreneurs. The local council has enlisted the services of a PR agency

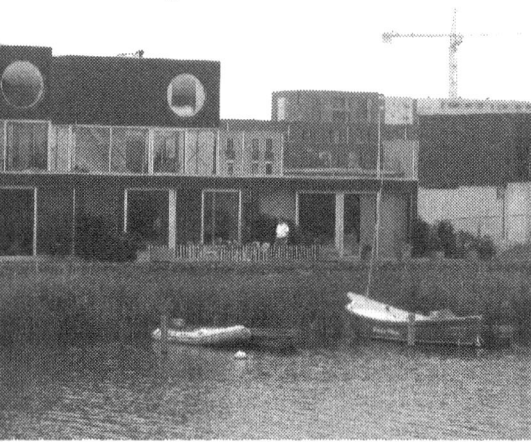

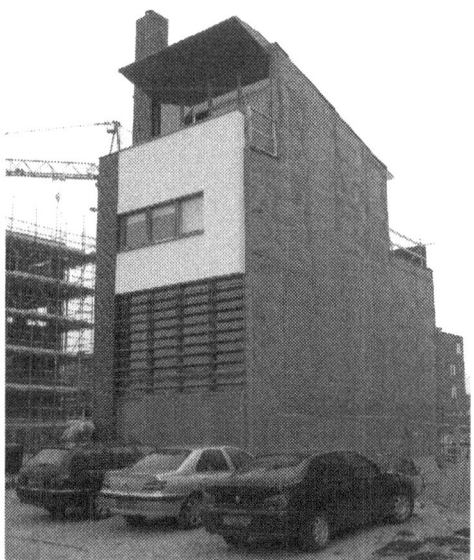

which distributes a colourful glossy. Leafing through its pages, you will see images only of white people – in an area where 70 out of every 100 inhabitants are first or second generation immigrants – telling you how beautiful their new houses are and praising the cultural activities in the neighbourhood. The real perversity starts when it becomes clear that the renewal plans openly state the intention of removing immigrant entrepreneurs from the neighbourhood. The plan literally reads 'the appearance of most of the shops leaves much to be desired. The number of migrant shop owners has grown drastically in the last couple of years.'[8]

Exclusive Inclusion

The local council wants more luxury shops and has started a 'discouragement policy' to remove Turkish grocery stores, coffeeshops and call shops from the main shopping street. While some policy makers mention growing immigrant entrepreneurship as a great success in the integration process, others perceive it as a problem to be solved by removal.

This is the new logic of inclusion and exclusion in urban renewal. In the I amsterdam model talent is sought after and social problems kept at bay. But again, the model is not restricted to Amsterdam: also Rotterdam is part of the avant-garde. With less marketing and more fanaticism, immigrants and lower income residents are slowly being removed from the inner city. It is

becoming less and less clear where all these 'problems' can eventually go. The Amsterdam city council's estimates show that by 2008 so many people will have had to leave their houses as a result of the regeneration process that the entire Amsterdam area does not have enough replacement social housing to re-accommodate them.

At the same time fewer houses are being developed than promised. In July 2005 the local newspaper carried a claim by a real estate broker that the council has consciously fostered a housing shortage. Now that the upward course of the housing market is slowly abating, the strange consequence is that the council has an interest in keeping a housing shortage in place to guarantee a good price for the new houses produced by the city's redevelopment.[9] The policy is creating a situation where council statistics themselves show that the official primary target group of the housing policy – those on lower incomes – are the people with the smallest chance of actually finding social housing. The main victims of the continuing housing shortage are predominantly immigrant families and youth. For them I amsterdam is a highly exclusive brand.

Postscript

In the west of the city, where one of the biggest redevelopment projects in Europe is being realised, the process has stalled. In this area, which due to its size

Image: M.O.

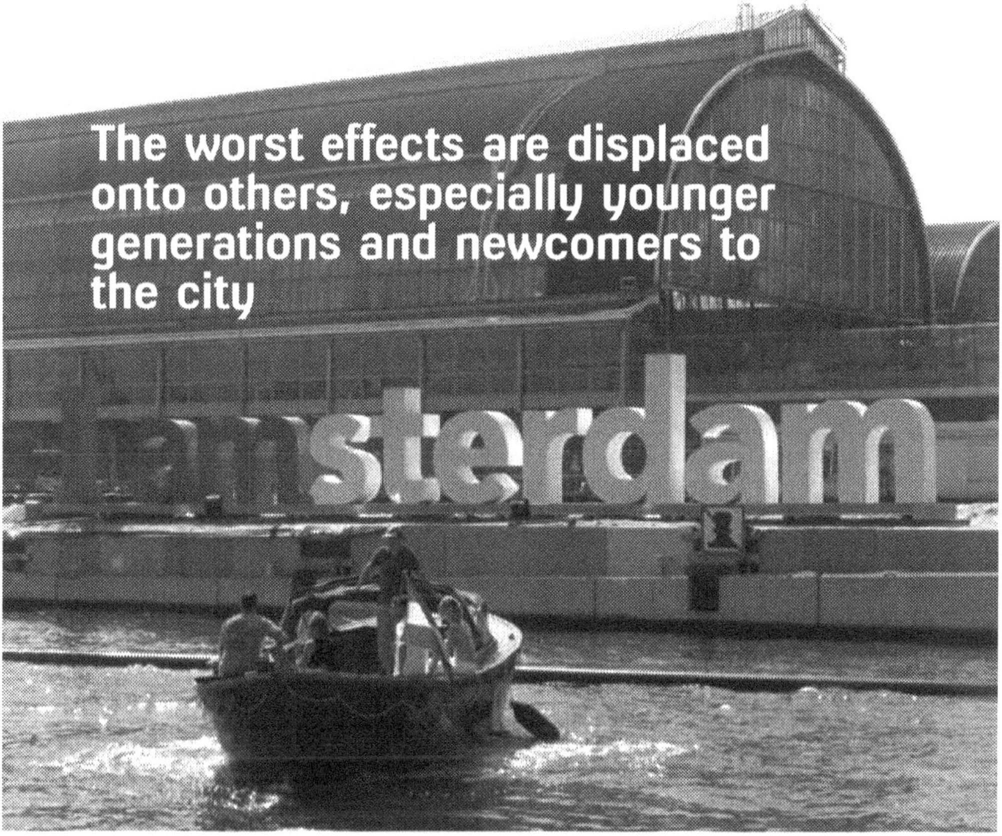

Merijn Oudenampsen

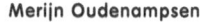

The worst effects are displaced onto others, especially younger generations and newcomers to the city

serves as a role model for other developments, it turns out the market has its limitations after all. Middle class interest in the poor neighbourhood and its newly constructed owner-occupant apartments is lower than expected, most turn out to prefer single family dwellings. The new challenge for the scheme's designers is to concentrate as many of the original occupants as possible in high density constructions, while leaving luscious green space for the more private and expensive housing. What will assist the process is that the city council, in financial distress, has outsourced neighbourhood participation schemes and decision making to the housing corporations. In general, statistics show that most of the people staying behind in the neighbourhood's residual social housing have not benefited from renewal as promised. The continuing social-economic problems in depressed neighbourhoods limit the marketability of space, forcing the city council to reconsider commencing social investment programmes. The renewal in west Amsterdam so far has turned out to be an economic and social failure. ✒

Footnotes

1

Rapport Woonvisie Amsterdam, http://www.dienst-wonen.nl

2

The Netherlands is blessed with a very big social housing sector. Here's some essential info: in Amsterdam roughly 70 percent of housing is rented and 50 percent of this is social housing. To apply for social housing you have to wait in line. The queue in Amsterdam has grown to a mean waiting period of 7.5 years. This is partly because a large quantity of middle income people live in social housing. Outside of social housing there is almost no genuinely affordable rental housing. Those that are forced to leave their homes due to urban renewal are given general priority on the waiting list, and specific priority to get a home in their original neighbourhood. However, due to the fact that the amount of social housing in any given redevelopment area is decreasing, there is not that much choice. A lot of the ex-inhabitants end up on the periphery of the city, where housing is still relatively cheap and often also more spacious. Usually they have to face an increase in rents.

3

For examples of the approaches to urban regeneration Amsterdam is taking, borrowing extensively from UK ideologues, see the conference Creative Capital: Culture, Innovation and the Public Domain in the Knowledge Economy, Amsterdam, March 17 and 18 2005, http://www.creativecapital.nl

4

Sail is a big maritime event, basically a parade of large sailing boats old and new through the city harbour. Most of the boats are hired by the Amsterdam business community to hold receptions.

5

Maakbaarheid is not an easily translated concept: 'the ability to shape, form and control every aspect of the social and physical environment; the belief that a country can be planned or made'. A modernist and progressive notion that in common Dutch understanding is believed to have died somewhere shortly after the '70s.

6
Schaefer was a famous Amsterdam alderman who vigorously coordinated the urban renewal wave in the late '70s and '80s. 'Bouwen voor de buurt' literally 'building for the neighbourhood' was a policy whereby urban renewal was specifically tailored to the needs of the original inhabitants of the neighbourhood and allowed them to return after the construction works.

7
Until recently gentrification was only a very limited phenomenon in the Dutch housing market. Most poor neighbourhoods consisted mainly of social housing and were thus protected by law. With the privatisation of housing corporations and minister Dekker's social mixing agenda, gentrification has now become part of the official housing policy.

8
See page 32 of the Stedelijk Vernieuwingsplan Indische Buurt.

9
The mean price of a house in the Netherlands has grown from €61,000 in 1985 to €224,000 in 2005; a rise of 367 percent.

Merijn Oudenampsen
<merijn.o@gmx.net> is part of the Dutch critical platform Flexmens,
http://www.flexmens.org
He has been involved in organising political projects and debates around flexibility and precarity. Currently he is writing a thesis on 'creative' city branding, entrepreneurialism and gentrification in Amsterdam

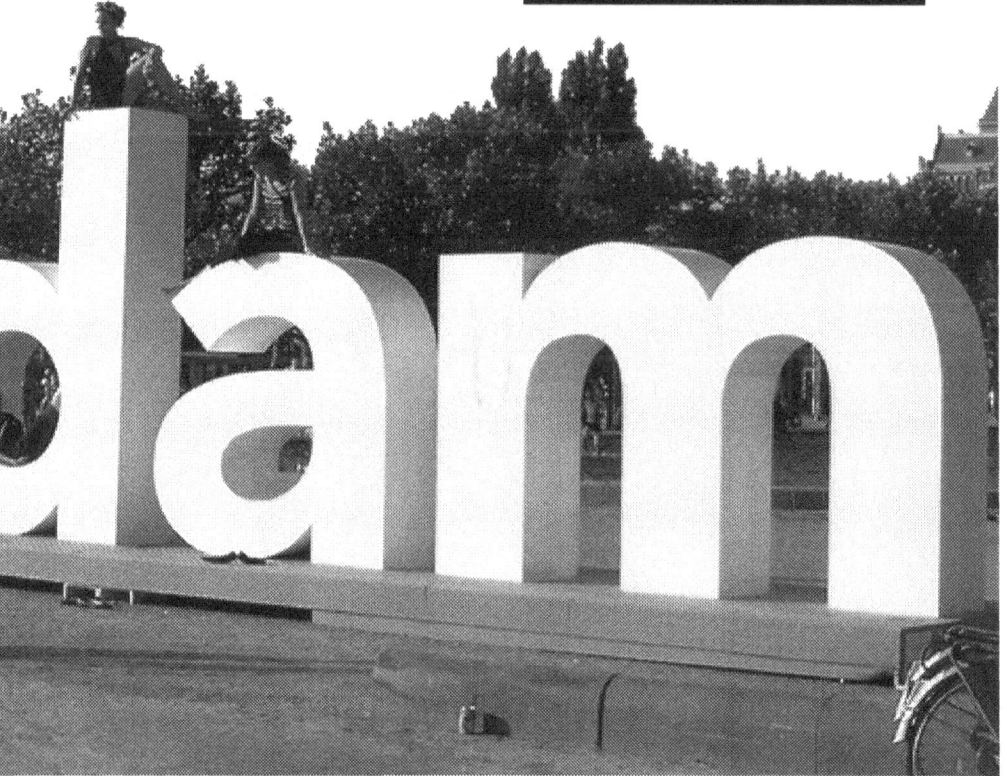

Image: M.O.

READER FLATTERY: IAIN SINCLAIR AND THE COLONISATION OF EAST LONDON

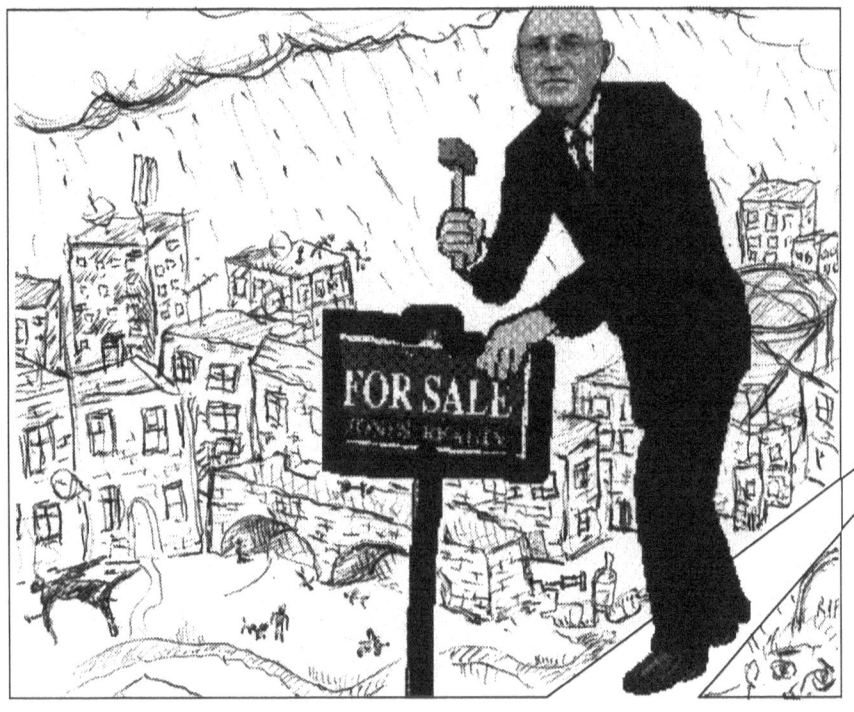

by John Barker

Image: by the Gimp

Iain Sinclair is familiar as a psychogeographic chronicler of London's East End in transition from Dickensian darkness to socially cleansed sterility. But is he an enemy of the urban enclosures or a literary estate agent, a seer or a voyeur? John Barker offers a stylistic analysis and some embedded psychogeographic reportage of his own

A longer version of this text is available on the *Mute* website:
http://metamute.org/en/reader-flattery

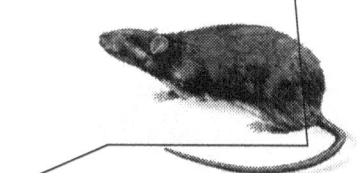

The colonisation of East London by the rich and their functionaries had begun well before the appearance of Iain Sinclair's fictions *White Chappell, Scarlet Tracings* and *Downriver* in which the area itself is the main character. But the colonisation and class cleansing has proceeded apace since then. My contention is that Sinclair has aided it in small measure by the bohemian ambience he has given East London in his work, one written in a relentless wiseguy prose full of false drama, from a rebel persona, that has grown increasingly unbelievable. It is a style that gives no space to, and yet flatters the reader.

In the process Sinclair has lost his raw material, and his more recent work has spread out geographically, but he has also done a slick job of pulling up the drawbridge after him. East London psychogeography is now passé: been there, done that. Though he would probably be outraged by the suggestion, given his scorn for the first wave of colonisers, Sinclair has not just lost his material but contributed to the loss. There is such a thing as the unintended consequence. There is the famous case of another Sinclair, Upton. His novel *The Jungle* had the intention of improving working conditions in the Chicago stockyards, but its effect was to horrify the bourgeoisie about the meat they bought and produced as a result the Federal Food and Drug Agency.

The unintended consequence may arise simply from a lack of self-awareness. In Iain Sinclair's case there is evidence of such a lack when it comes to the style and most of all, the tone of his writing. To get some sense of this, and the wiseguy nature of the prose without reference to East London itself, here is Sinclair reviewing Tom Raworth's *Collected Poems* in the *London Review of Books*.[1] He's a big fan and by way of contrast he attacks Martin Amis' use of 'like' to introduce:

> a well-turned simile from a Martian verse-maker. Raworth, and those who have learned from him don't do similes.

Already there are the wiseguy giveaways, the 'Martian' from Martin and the 'don't do'. The problem with similes, as Sinclair goes on to say, is that they 'diminish narrative integrity' by suggesting that this work, this map, is not in itself convincing or true. The simile says: applaud my wit. Yes indeed, similes should be used sparingly, if at all, but a paragraph or two later, Sinclair himself indulges in one simile after another in remorseless fashion after his pompous pronouncement that 'we can't afford to ignore Raworth'. These similes have a heavy tread:

– but the politics have evaporated like a puddle on hot tarmac
– his father's letter like a shimmering 8mm home movie
– staying on the case like a disenfranchised private eye

This lack of self-awareness runs right through his East End fictions where he, perhaps unwittingly, uses a variety of modes that 'diminish narrative integrity'. But first, a sketch of how inner London, and East London especially, had changed before Sinclair took it as material.

The First Wave

Well into the 1970s, much of inner London was still poor London, full of council housing and private rented flats and bedsits. However, there was also a process of colonisation which began with the opening of the Victoria Line at the end of the 1960s. The first wave of gentrification happened at the very time when a bohemian lifestyle became more of a mass option and inner London was the place to be.

East London psychogeography is passé: been there, done that

Rental properties became owner-occupied houses or flats, causing a steep rise in house prices and rents, so that already by 1974 *The Financial Times* could headline 'Housing's Arithmetic of Despair'. Margaret Thatcher's government policies on council housing accelerated the process.

These factors were common to the class cleansing across London but East London has its own special history, a place of interest to writers, social reformers, and voyeurs with always a hint of the dangerous. It has a history of immigrations; radical politics with at least two waves of property squatting; and militant trade unionism both in the docks and at Ford Dagenham. East End 'gentrification' began in Spitalfields with its Huguenot houses and Wapping with its warehouses. These Victorian (and earlier) buildings lost their original function with the closure of the London docks as containerisation allowed a shift to ports on the coast. This gave a jump-start to class-cleansing, smashing the base of labour militancy and releasing hundreds of acres of real estate onto the market. House prices were not improved, however. They have since been relentlessly pushed up (unless an area was deemed too naff, dangerous, or aesthetically displeasing) by a variety of factors:

– proximity to the City of London labour market and that of the socially engineered Canary Wharf
– the Europe-wide dynamic of artists looking for cheap rents, making an area attractive and then being pushed out by the consequent rent rises
– well-off parents putting up mortgage deposits or buying housing outright for their children
– their professionalisation of the bohemian lifestyle

These are 'objective' conditions, but in his own way, in the form of reader flattery, Sinclair has helped the process along.

Ripping Yarns

Spitalfields has been a constant centre of interest for Sinclair. For a brief period in 1979 I swept its streets. At that time my round began with a dead rat or two in the gutters of Sheba Street, a tenement that ran parallel to Brick Lane, which itself had to be defended from the National Front. No regrets that either of those has gone, but the changed demography is visible in the shrinkage of the Lane's Sunday morning 'flea market', and the explosion of property prices. The area also had a long-term morbid attraction as Jack the Ripper territory, the streets in which six prostitutes – the very word still a vicarious thrill in today's media world – were murdered. They were killings for which no one was charged or convicted. But such is the gaslight and myth attraction of this sordid affair that tourist guides walk parties of tourists around the sites of each of the six killings. In the autumn of 1988 a group of women began to picket such tours. By then Sinclair's *White Chappell, Scarlet Tracings* was emerging from its small press publication (Goldmark) in 1987 to a wider audience. Of the various possible Jacks, one, the surgeon Sir William Gull, is a main thread in the book. Sinclair, with his usual cast of bohemians (no admission to book dealers who aren't crazed one way or another), is quick to let it be known that his rehash of these sexist murders is not going to be the usual vulgar stuff. Oh no.

> The zone was gradually defined, the labyrinth penetrated. It was given limits by the victims of the Ripper.

Nothing vulgar, but a false sense of drama, one that 'diminishes the narrative integrity', is immediately created by the use of 'labyrinth' and 'zone', a word lifted from the paranoid and angry views of reality of William Burroughs and Thomas Pynchon. 'Zone' rather than the streets where tossers emptied their ashtrays into the gutter of my Brick Lane patch. Just in case we've missed the point, that this is not run of the mill Ripperism, he has his bohemian oppo, Jobling, say of another Ripper book:

> There's something inherently seedy and salacious in continually picking off the scabs of those crimes, peering at mutilated corpses, listing the undergarments, trekking over the tainted ground in quest of some long-delayed occult frisson.

None of that for Sinclair and Jobling, though they are not immune to a bit of 'long-delayed occult frisson' themselves both here and in the recycling of the David Rodinsky story. And there's a falsity to the rhetoric, there can be no peering at corpses because there are none. But Sinclair is determined that their take on the myth is on a higher, offbeat, plane, one in which they will reverse the conventions of detective fiction:

Our narrative starts everywhere. We want to assemble all the incomplete movements, like cubists, until the point is reached where the crime can commit itself. That is why there are so many Ripper candidates, so many theories: and they can all be right.

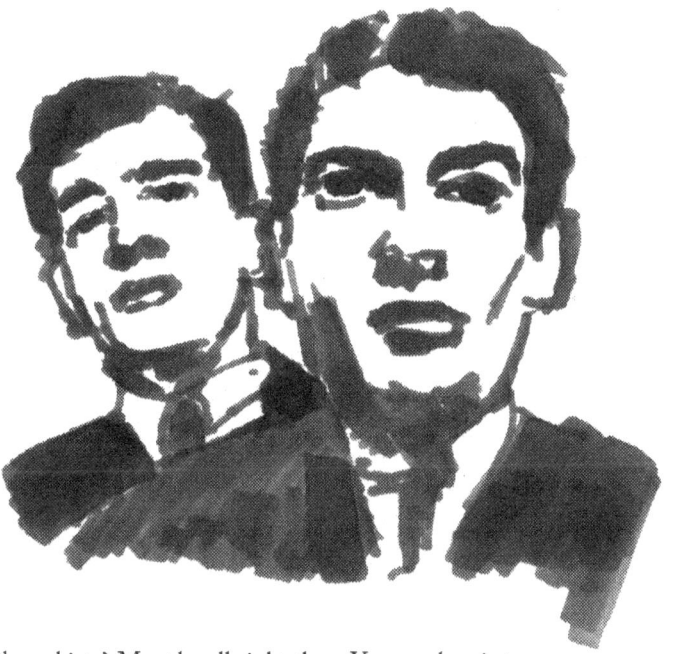

Like cubists? Must be all right then. You can buy into East London myth and not feel mucky, neither a tourist nor a tabloid reader. Not naff at all.[2]

Wankers

In this same first novel, something more familiar is at work in making East London both exciting and safe for the modern bourgeois with a taste for the off-beat: it is the rhetoric of disgust. Its tone was set in T.S. Eliot's vastly overrated poem *The Wasteland*, and is all too easy to do, far more difficult to write joy and pleasure. Here is a taste of it from Sinclair on a stretch of unmarked passage to Limehouse Reach:

Image: Esiri Erheriene-
Essithe, the Kray twins

> Maps of futility brought to ground … There's nowhere to
> drink here: the pubs collapsed into their own pretensions,
> understudy villains ordering up cocktail froth, the mind-
> destroying jingle of electronic pickpockets.

The giveaway here are those 'understudy villains'. What are they
then? Pretend villains? Ones who just aren't up to it? Either way
a wanker, vulgar too, drinking his cocktail froth. This before the
very heavy tread of 'mind-destroying jingle of electronic
pickpockets' as a description of fruit machines.

In his attack on Martin Amis cited above, Sinclair uses him
as a prime example of the same strategy:

> Critical consensus and broad readership made their
> choice long ago, stick with satire, smartly observed
> behaviourist rants (trashing the proles), small revenges.

Attacks on Amis strengthen one's own position as a rebel in
the cultural world, and here Sinclair's attack is spot on. The
trouble is that, as with the similes, Sinclair does so much of
the same stuff himself. We can see it in his use of a different

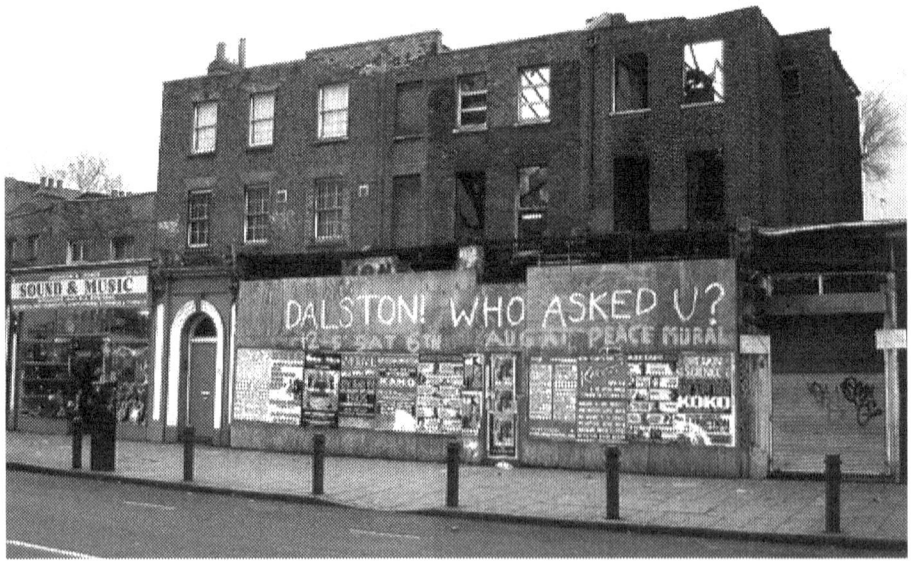

Image: Fin Fahey,
http://flickr.com
(thanks, Web 2.0)

Sinclair lets us know that his rehash of these sexist murders is not going to be the usual vulgar stuff. Oh no

East London almost mythical heritage, its criminals, the Kray twins especially. He can't let them alone so we get an endless cycle of parading, then trashing these faces from the past. His account of Ronnie Kray's funeral in *Lights Out for the Territory* from 1997 begins with a characteristic self-dramatisation: 'It was quite a trick blagging my way through the crowd', one made up of 'the jobless, the unwaged, the never haves, the ones who parrot the party line, and the ones who don't have the faintest idea what's going on today or any other day.'

By the time of this book, Sinclair was a well established and acclaimed writer. Blagging? Really? I don't think so, though he has made much of how he has got himself into the funeral parlour with 'a mangled bookseller's card used for claiming discounts'. Wow. In all probability they didn't give a monkey's who he was. And what is this crowd he has blagged through? Wankers, all of them. Wankers of different stripes, but that's what they

are, including those who 'parrot the party line'. Here it is the verb, parrot, which is so value-laden. And, what party line is that? The nostalgia party, the good old East End, that one? The ones given substance by the crowd of geezers who he is just waiting to wrap up in a put-down:

> Villains that are so old they think they're being flash by giving two fingers to petrol rationing.

He likes this so much we get another of his triplet sentences where it is all summed up.

> This has been a major killing for the car rental mob, the muscle agencies, the three-chair barbers.

'Mob?' Hertz and Avis?

It is the funeral as spectacle he can't stand, that's the line, but he comes back to it, years later, in *Dining on Stones*, because it's such good material for the phrases that sum it all up for us, so that we too can patronise the whole thing:

> Adios neighbourhood heavies …
> the old firms were good for
> nothing except heritage TV:
> suits and wreaths at Chingford
> Mount, gravel-voiced killers
> schmoozing the camera …
> Respects were offered, upper
> case carnations by the serial
> mourners of gangland: Freddie
> Foreman, Tony Lambrianou …

In other words, more wankers. Except I remember Freddie
Foreman clearly. The first time he ever took a tab of acid and
laughed at the screw who was banging up. That was 1974 in D
Wing when it was the max security wing of Wormwood Scrubs.
Then, some months later, Fred decking this giant of a culchie
screw on the eve of his first ever home leave in 8 years;
whacking him because the screw had been giving grief to Gerry
Kelly, now MP for North Belfast, all evening long.

But it is not just East London's pensioner criminals,
whatever you think of them, who get the Sinclair treatment.
This is him in *Downriver* where at dawn in a lorry car park, he
sees girls dropping down from lorry cabs.

> The girls were inevitably overweight with make-up
> scattered like an autistic action painting; or scrawny,
> nerve-ticked, scratched, pimpled and frantic to score,
> wriggling in satin, torn fish-net, split and smeared
> saddle-leather.

It's pretty obvious what kind of girls these are. These are
proles, and ugly with it, ugly and pathetic. It starts with the
make-up simile, and then goes into one judgemental adjective
after another – boy does he pile it on – interspersed for variety
with the value-leaden verb, 'wriggling'. And it is hard to see
how it is different from Amis, here with some early
description of Keith Talent in *London Fields*:

> Keith's crowning glory, his hair, was thick and full
> bodied: but it always had the look of having been
> recently washed, imperfectly rinsed, and then, still slick
> with cheap shampoo, slow-dried in a huddled pub ...

The distinctive value-laden adverb 'imperfectly' followed by
the adjective that you just know it is going to be 'cheap'.
Notoriously, he goes on to give him more of a kicking:

> You don't need much empathic talent to tell what
> Keith's thinking. He doesn't do that much thinking in
> the first place. The very difficulty, the disuse of the

muscles, writes headlines on his forehead, and his
tabloid face.

Which is him summed up, wrapped up, and placed across the
counter. But how is this different to Sinclair on dog owners:

> The pit-bull is twinned in desirability with the
> possession of a satellite dish … the Dog and Dish, they
> hang out together, chummy as a pub sign

Or in the same book, Sinclair on a bus giving us the dope on
its passengers:

> The willingly bemused, a troop of dope swollen moon
> faces, the sort usually glimpsed as they stare out of
> yellow, special needs minibuses with lifts at the back. I'm
> sure we've infiltrated a secure-hospital delivery, a round-
> up of sectioned carpet-chewers, white line stalkers,
> parrot imitators, biddable psychotics, folks who live with
> the daily horror of seeing things as they actually are.

The style is more hyper than Amis, the piling on of phrases, but
the effect is the same. And at the end of this passage he gives us
his own version of T.S. Eliot's cheek and pomposity in the
famous line from *The Four Quartets*, 'Human kind cannot bear
very much reality.' To which one can only say, speak for yourself.

Crazies

This passage occurs as part of one of Sinclair's necessarily
offbeat searches and following of trails. East London becomes
a playground of weird connections. In the bus sequence he is
in search of an obscure psychogeographer at work in an
obscure room in the University of Greenwich with some
absurd, self-imposed deadline. These searches are invariably
given a drama of their own. Sometimes he uses an additional
method of 'diminishing narrative integrity' to achieve this. The
first person present tense functions as an A to B method of
generating excitement:

Easily into our stride, I'm explaining the whole insane concept to Marc: on the hoof. No time for maps and bearings … Spoken out loud, put into words, our journey sounds insane. It *is* insane.

More often the excitement is generated by those triplets of verbs: back with poor David Rodinsky again; 'We dug, we competed, we whispered our discoveries', just as his hyper- book dealers do throughout his work. As well as Rodinsky, the Ripper comes back to provide more weird connection material:

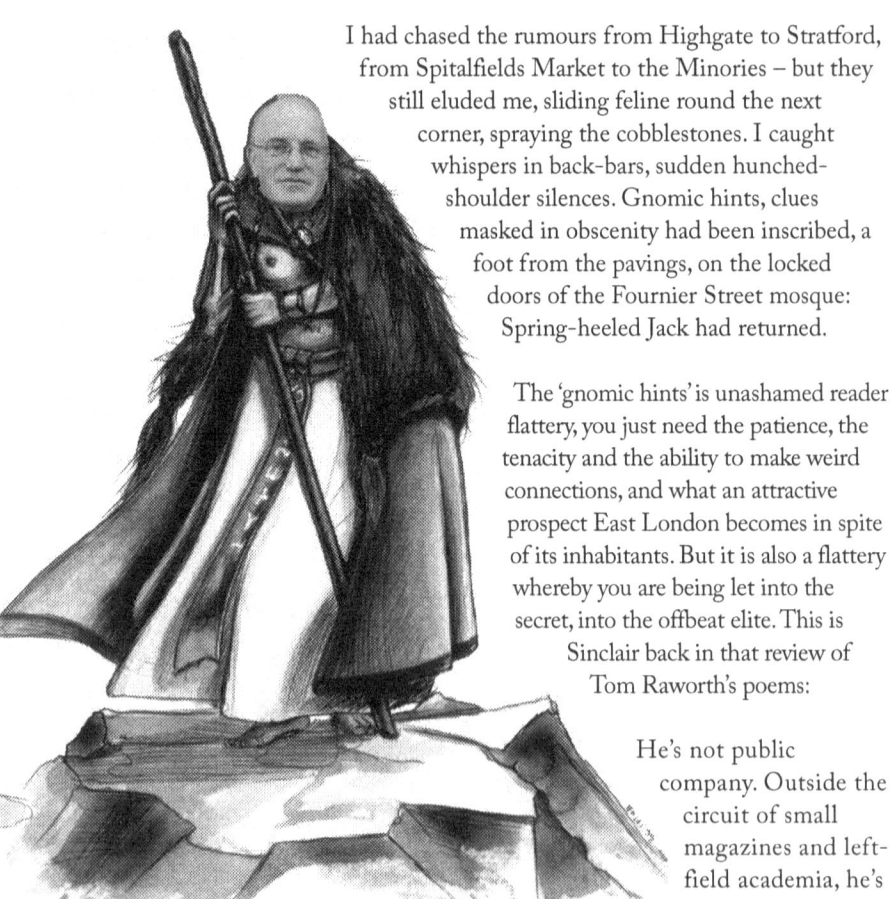

I had chased the rumours from Highgate to Stratford, from Spitalfields Market to the Minories – but they still eluded me, sliding feline round the next corner, spraying the cobblestones. I caught whispers in back-bars, sudden hunched-shoulder silences. Gnomic hints, clues masked in obscenity had been inscribed, a foot from the pavings, on the locked doors of the Fournier Street mosque: Spring-heeled Jack had returned.

The 'gnomic hints' is unashamed reader flattery, you just need the patience, the tenacity and the ability to make weird connections, and what an attractive prospect East London becomes in spite of its inhabitants. But it is also a flattery whereby you are being let into the secret, into the offbeat elite. This is Sinclair back in that review of Tom Raworth's poems:

He's not public company. Outside the circuit of small magazines and left-field academia, he's not news.

Image: by the Gimp

Seen from the outside, how easy to make those wonderful nights sound naff

Or worse, a recent piece in *Guardian Weekend*, 18 March, 2006, on the huge car boot sales at Hackney Wick. He writes of the photographer Stephen Gill who 'had stumbled on one of the great secrets of the city.' Great secret? When the parked cars reach back to Homerton High Street on a Sunday morning? And there's a predictability to the photographer using a 50p camera and Sinclair talking of 'provisional zones'.

Sometimes, as in the case of the Edith Cadiz story in *Downriver*, there were moments when 'The trail was cold'. This story uses gothic Hackney Hospital for its location and of this he writes:

> I would adopt my usual method, and circumnavigate the hospital walls; see what the stones had to say. The hospital … had in the meantime, been the designated dumping ground for all the swamp-field crazies, the ranters, the ultimate referrals.

The triplet of hyped-up phrases that concludes the passage is familiar, its summing-up tone, more important is the use to which Sinclair puts the hospital itself. *Downriver* came out in 1991, the year also of Dr David Widgery's *Some Lives: A GP's East End*. In this book he talks of how painful it is to be 'called to a person who has died unattended and alone.' And mentions how in 1990, a 91-year-old demented man lay dead in the grounds of Hackney Hospital for three weeks before discovery. I am not making any claims for social realism as against imaginative attempts to give a picture of a place. I do not myself believe Margaret Thatcher is a witch, but that she was a clever politician with a nasty agenda for which there was a historical opportunity. Despite this, I find Sinclair's writing is at its best when it is unashamedly mystical, when he goes for it without covering his arse in advance. What I find difficult, in addition to the reader flattery, and the knowing summings-up, is that there are no ordinary East Enders in his East End.

Widgery is neither sentimental nor nostalgic, it is already in 1990 a new East End:

> Cockney individualism, far from vanishing as Ian Nairn feared, has become still more diverse if less obvious with the wild adaptations made by a multicultural proletariat and a sizeable bohemia.

Here the doctor, a free-thinking socialist, is inclusive in welcoming a new East London, bohemians and all. For Sinclair however, only bohemians count. The multicultural proletariat appears only in summing-up phrases, or as crazies. In *Lights Out*, for example, there are no black people except for a bag lady on Queensbridge Road, and an incompetent mini cab driver at the end. Instead, as in *Downriver*, Hackney Wick exists only as the house of a crazed drunken aristocrat, Elgin MacDiarmuid, and is seen only from this point of view, a house turned over by

> Barrio-rats and spike-skulled squatters from distressed chip-vans.

Wow! More crazies in their parcels.

Sinclair is ahead of this game too. One of his other handy punchbags are TV guys in search of the offbeat, and he can be very funny, Situationist style, on this world. One of them tells him:

> Go for those nutty characters you write about; off the wall eccentrics, headbangers with chutzpah ... Dig them out and we'll shoot them ... Give me that surreal, subhuman cartoon feel you're so good at.

But this doesn't prevent him of giving us precisely such material over-and-over-again. In Widgery's account, madness is a very miserable business, as are all kinds of alcohol and chemical abuse. His is not a book full of saints. Along with the long-suffering folk who don't go for medical help early enough because they didn't want to make a fuss, there are manipulators and the violent, and mothers finding it harder than they'd thought. The chapter 'Visitations' is pretty hard going emotionally. But he can still write, a socialist without the notorious rose-coloured specs:

> Still, what strikes me about all those condescending documentaries about the poor East Enders, ignorant, ill and probably racist into the bargain, is exactly the reverse: how well the modern Cockneys do in circum-stances which their 'betters' would find impossible ... And yet how much more common decency, respect for humanity, honour and humour they possess than so

many of the middle and upper classes who despite lip service to collective values in fact approach life in a spirit of naked self-interest.

First Among Psychogeographers

If Sinclair is not self-aware when it comes to the style of much of his writing, it is because those value-laden summing-ups are so ingrained in the tradition passed down from Eliot, who Sinclair quotes regularly. What he cleverly knits this together with is a style that on the surface seems so antithetical to the Eliot view of the world. It is the psychogeographical style with a situationist edge which suits the business of trails and searches. Once it had a subversive sting but it has become a stuck-in-time aesthetic. In *Lights Out,* Sinclair stands up for it:

> Drifting purposefully is the recommended mode ... To the no bullshit materialist this sounds suspiciously like *fin de siècle* decadence, a poetic of entropy – but the born again *flaneur* is a stubborn creature, less interested in texture and fabric, eavesdropping on philosophical conversation pieces, than in noticing everything. Alignments of telephone kiosks, maps made from the moss on the slopes of Victorian sepulchres, collections of prostitute's cards, torn and defaced promotional bills for cancelled events at York Hall ...

The possible criticism is, then, absorbed, dealt with in advance. But what a big deal he makes of it in contrast, say, to the great exiled Greek anarchist and historian Elias Petroupolis with his histories of Greek public toilets, bars, cemeteries, songs and more.

By the time of *Dining on Stones*, the criticism has not just been absorbed in advance, the veteran has seen it, done it, and comments:

> Locally my wanderings were interrupted by cyclists eager to tell me about their projects: video surveillance of empty buildings, albums of re-photographed graffiti, underground streams tracked to source.

This doesn't prevent him from bringing the Ripper back in yet again before going on to trash it as old hat once more.

> Brick Lane was a permanent exhibition of look-at-me-graphics, stencils, retro-Situationism ...

You can only admire the chutzpah of this non-headbanger, this writer of look-at-me prose. Chutzpah was something on offer from non-retro-situationism. I was greatly influenced by the situationists in the late 1960s. There was a cockiness to their style that we needed at the time, but cockiness too can become a clichéd rhetoric. Brian Holmes has wondered how the situationist 'aesthetic' has maintained its prestige in such dramatically different times, and when they had themselves been recuperated in the 1980s with a situationist exhibition at the Pompidou Centre. In the case of Sinclair, it is because it allows him to have it both ways: it allows him to be snooty about both the big money and the offbeat bourgeois of the first wave of colonisation. This is him in full flow against the recuperators in *Downriver*:

> 'Baroque realists' and tame voyeurs fixated on entropy, tremble in paroxysms of excitement and distaste. There hasn't been such hot material lying around in the streets since they nobbled public hangings and bear baiting. Suddenly we're all Henry Mayhew and Jack London. It's shudder – unbelievable, terrible. We rush to our word processors, the hot line to Channel 4. We're going to get the lead story, with photograph, in the *London Review of Books*.

Chutzpah? You have to admire the way he does it. Not just that he is a regular in *London Review of Books*, it's that 'we'. He's part of it, but he's not part of it, because he was there first and is aware of what's happening. Aware, and not aware, because it's what he does so often in the writing: 'paroxysms of excitement and distaste'. And when it comes to anger at docklands development – 'the seriously wealthy river-spivs' – it comes as a riff (Part 8 of *Downriver*) in which a comic-strip

Margaret Thatcher born out of Queen Victoria wants a memorial built in docklands, for which there must be a committee. This allows for a souped-up satire of the spectacle in which some of his favourite targets appear, like the architectural advisor 'selling bijou residences in Cherry Gardens to half-solvent media lefties' and who found it 'a real drag dealing with social climbing paupers,' and promises of 'retrospective justifications' and 'prime time television'.

Once upon a time, such a style could carry a punch as in Ishmael Reed's work, and especially *Mumbo-Jumbo*, where it is able to carry Reed's anger. For the last 25 years or so in the Western world, however, you have to wonder if 'savage satire' isn't an oxymoron, the savagery impossible especially in such wiseguy prose. Sinclair seems clear about this in the case of Martin Amis but for himself, his outlook seems to be of the better-dead-than-naff variety. Compare the docklands memorial satire of *Downriver* to Chapter 10 of David Widgery's book, 'Consequences'. Here, some very unsentimental stories of heroes, non-heroes, and sickness, intercut with what the London Docklands Development Corporation is doing on the day Canary Wharf is 'topped out'. Tenants are 'decanted' from St Vincent House and Risby House to make way for its infrastructure, and the architect of that Fat Canary says:

A skyscraper recognises that by virtue of its height it has acquired civic responsibilities. We expect it to have formal characteristics appropriate for this unique and socially charged role.

Reality outdoing any satire, as Tom Lehrer said, giving it up when Henry Kissinger was awarded a Nobel Peace Prize.

Reassuringly Authentic

The colonising of East London did not stop with Wapping, Limehouse basin or Canary Wharf. It has extended not just geographically but in the manner that enclosures tend to do, culturally. In Hackney, it is most visible, and hurtful, in the disappearance in the last few years of at least four big pubs where the crack was fierce and wild. Public houses, public spaces. And they are going, the ones where there was some freedom to the public space. First down was The Albion to the north of the borough. A big old Victorian affair that served a sub-culture of goths and mohicans, many of whom were stalwarts of that anti-capitalist movement on the streets. It is now large-scale apartments. As is the Pembury Tavern at the Amhurst Road end of the Pembury Estate. A pub where they didn't bother too much with furniture. The music changed but it was always loud.

Further along at the top end of Mare Street was the Samuel Pepys where a really fine band might turn up out of the blue and where you'd hear where that night's squatted rave was happening, and then get asked by the 20-year-old on the door – humiliating this – if you was the law. Now reclaimed by the landlords, The Hackney Empire, and sterilised into an empty chrome and glass bar.

Sinclair does not come across as much of a pub man, the odd manic pint with manic book dealers or manic artists perhaps, and then be put off by all that cocktail froth, or an old dockers pub which gets the full disgust treatment with the leadweight irony of 'authentic', in *Dining on Stones*:

> The ham rolls were reassuringly authentic: crusted in over-tanned plaster of Paris, concealing a pink slick of reconstituted animal fat … the wallpaper had not been pasted to the wall: it had grown like a fungus. And was growing still.

Where there is a long pub scene, The Spear of Destiny in *Downriver*, it is full of Irish and Scots geezers beating shit out of each other in the public bar, and parcelled up in Sinclair phrases. It also has a literary ring to it, the landlord and his wife seeming to come out of *The Angel and the Cuckoo*, a novel by Gerald Kersh (a writer we both admire). The pub also has a snug bar where landlord Count Jerzy's wife keeps it cosy with the inscribed portraits of East End heroes and 'assorted bracelet-wearing gangsters', the sort he just can't leave alone, who must be shown to be wankers over and over again.

Worst of all in the Hackney pub clear-out was the closing of the Crown and Castle, on the corner of Dalston Lane and Kingsland Road, to become an eat in/eat out place, part of a chain. On weekend nights the place was mental. A DJ playing to a room of punters aged between 20 and 60, black and white, and the Hassidic guy who loved dancing with the big black women. We danced packed tight, rush-hour style, and for a few hours it was sexy as hell.

Seen from the outside, in summing-up phrases, how easy to make those wonderful nights sound naff. How tempting for someone writing in the Sinclair mode. In *Lights Out* he does it himself:

Dalston coming into its pomp after a railway carve-up, as an alternative for those who couldn't afford the trip 'up west', has all the buzz of a J.G. Ballard traffic island squatted by cowboys.

What a bloody cheek!

Yes, Sinclair does bear some responsibility for the incessant colonial process. Reading him, the colonisers can feel good about themselves and also enjoy this history-packed area of the city because now they know the score. The reader is flattered, he/she for sure is not one of the wankers, uglies, or phoneys who have been so exhaustively parcelled up for their enjoyment.

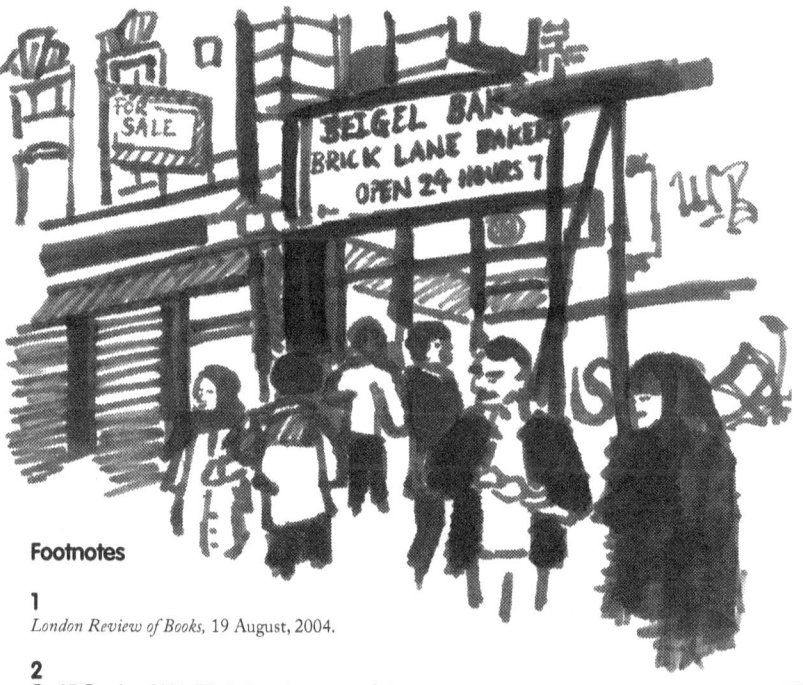

Footnotes

1
London Review of Books, 19 August, 2004.

2
On 27 October, 2001, *The Independent* reported that egg throwing and air rifle fire had taken place against tourists following Jack the Ripper's footsteps. They talked of 'cowboy' operators. It has become a real broadsheet standby, the 'cowboy' operator, gangmaster, dodgy builders and the rest. It is also one of those value-laden words much favoured by Sinclair. How about cowboy journalists, or cowboy consultants?

John Barker <harrier@easynet.co.uk> was born in London and works as a book indexer. His prison memoir *Bending the Bars* was reviewed for *Mute* by Stewart Home

Image: Esiri Erheriene-Essi, Brick Lane

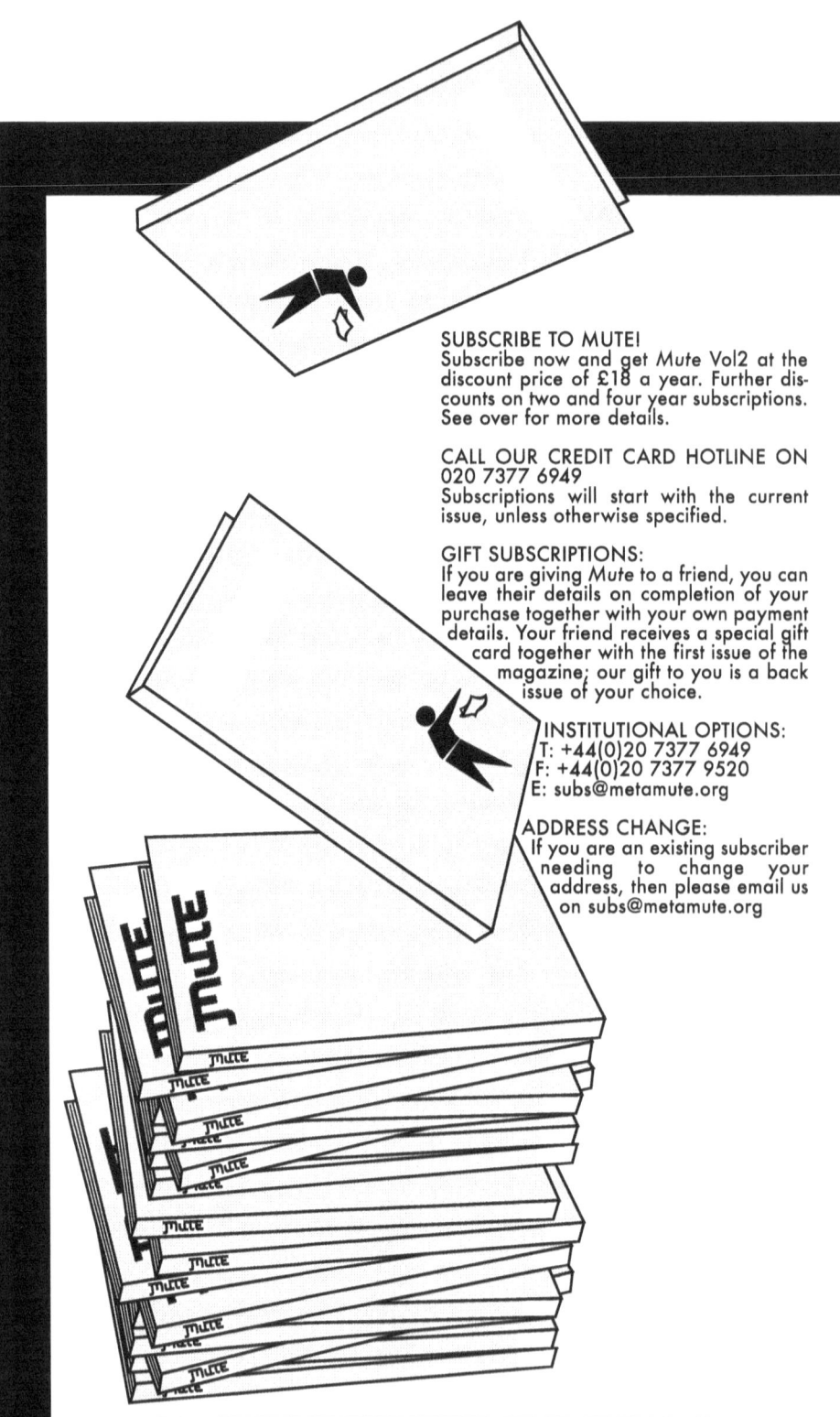

SUBSCRIBE TO MUTE!
Subscribe now and get Mute Vol2 at the discount price of £18 a year. Further discounts on two and four year subscriptions. See over for more details.

CALL OUR CREDIT CARD HOTLINE ON 020 7377 6949
Subscriptions will start with the current issue, unless otherwise specified.

GIFT SUBSCRIPTIONS:
If you are giving Mute to a friend, you can leave their details on completion of your purchase together with your own payment details. Your friend receives a special gift card together with the first issue of the magazine; our gift to you is a back issue of your choice.

INSTITUTIONAL OPTIONS:
T: +44(0)20 7377 6949
F: +44(0)20 7377 9520
E: subs@metamute.org

ADDRESS CHANGE:
If you are an existing subscriber needing to change your address, then please email us on subs@metamute.org

go to www.metamute.org/product

subscribe

Subscription Rates:

	individual		institutional/company	
	4 issues (1 year)	8 issues (2 years)	4 issues (1 year)	8 issues (2 years)
uk	☐ £18	☐ £34	☐ £27	☐ £51
eu	☐ €25	☐ €48	☐ €38	☐ €71
usa/can/mx	☐ $22	☐ $41	☐ $32	☐ $61
other	☐ €29	☐ €54	☐ €43	☐ €82

Please tick the appropriate box.

I wish to pay by cheque/credit card.
☐ I enclose a cheque (GBP) made payable to Mute.
☐ Please charge my

☐ Visa ☐ Access ☐ Mastercard ☐ Switch

Card no. ☐☐☐☐ ☐☐☐☐ ☐☐☐☐ ☐☐☐☐

Expiry date ☐☐ / ☐☐   Start date ☐☐ ☐☐

[Switch only] Issue number ☐☐

Signature _____

_____ name

_____ address

_____

_____ town/city

_____ post code

_____ country

POST TO:
MUTE, Unit 9, The Whitechapel Centre
85 Myrdle St., London E1 1HL, UK

Or call our credit card hotline 020 7377 6949,
Fax 020 7377 9520

Web http://www.metamute.org/product
Email mute@metamute.org

www.ingramcontent.com/pod-product-compliance
Lightning Source LLC
Chambersburg PA
CBHW030856180526
45163CB00004B/1603